"Rabbi Weiss, who was my student at the Academy for Jewish Religion, is to be commended for the sensitive and caring way that she treats those who have come to her seeking to learn more about Judaism (and in many cases join the Jewish people). She provides her students with a very positive view of religious observance, and exposes them to the richness of Orthodox tradition. I was quite pleased to learn that some of her students undergo an Orthodox conversion. Rabbi Weiss's infectious love of Judaism has no doubt been a great influence on the lives of the many who have sought her out. May G-d give her the strength and wisdom to continue her efforts to explain our beloved religion to those who are spiritually stranded and, like the king of the Khazars, seek to find truth and validity in the religious spheres of their lives."

—Rabbi Isaac H. Mann

faculty, Academy for Jewish Religion (Orthodox), New York

"Rabbi Bernice Weiss's book is an important and vital resource to inspire potential Jews by Choice and to help them resolve issues relating to personal identity, family conflicts and community. The book contains a series of powerful personal experiences of the contributors as they reflect the inner struggles and the unique adventures of becoming the children of Abraham and Sarah.

"This book is also an important resource for Jews by birth since it helps all of us to develop heightened sensitivities as we create formal ways and processes to ease their transition from being a non-Jew to the new status of being a Jew by Choice.

"I strongly believe that Rabbi Weiss's book will stimulate the reader's interest since it is invaluable to any member of the Jewish community who supports the compelling challenge of *Kayruv*—to welcome the much-needed and much-appreciated Jews by Choice into our People."

—Rabbi Seymour L. Essrog

past president, Rabbinical Assembly of America (Conservative)

Converting to Judaism

Choosing to Be Chosen

Personal Stories

RABBI BERNICE K. WEISS

with SHERIE LERNER SILVERMAN

SIMCHA PRESS
An Imprint of Health Communications, Inc.®

Deerfield Beach, Florida
www.simchapress.com

Library of Congress Cataloging-in-Publication Data

Converting to Judaism : choosing to be chosen : personal
stories / [compiled and edited by] Bernice K. Weiss with
Sherie Lerner Silverman.
    p.   cm.
  ISBN 1-55874-820-2 (pbk.)
  1. Jewish converts from Christianity—United States—
Biography.   I. Weiss, Bernice K., date.   II. Silverman,
Sherie Lerner.
BM729.P7 C69 2000
296.7'14'092273—dc21
[B]

                                                   00-058796

Simcha Press, its Logos and Marks are trademarks of Health
Communications, Inc.

Publisher: Simcha Press
              An Imprint of Health Communications, Inc.
              3201 S.W. 15th Street
              Deerfield Beach, FL 33442-8190

Cover design by Lisa Camp
Inside book design by Dawn Grove

To the Past—My Father and Mother,
Hyman and Lucille Kimel

To the Future—My Children,
Rachael, Jonathan and Stephanie

CONTENTS

ACKNOWLEDGMENTS

The first impetus to record my students' stories took shape with the aid of a Melton Senior Educators Fellowship for Jewish Education in the Diaspora, at Hebrew University in Jerusalem, during the years 1995 and 1996. The work of the Washington Institute for Conversion and the Study of Judaism, located in Rockville, Maryland, and the unfolding stories of my students as they discover Jewish life, have been made possible because of the support of mentors, scholars and friends.

I am thankful for the assistance and support of leaders in the Jewish community whose varied viewpoints reflect the pluralistic approach that guides my work: Dr. Michael Berenbaum, Professor of Theology (Adjunct), University of Judaism, Los Angeles, California; Rabbi Shear Yashuv Cohen, Chief Rabbi, Haifa, Israel; The Honorable Stuart E. Eizenstat, Deputy Secretary of the United States Department of the Treasury, Washington, D.C.; Rabbi Seymour Essrog, past president, Rabbinical Assembly of America; Rabbi Barry Freundel, Kesher Israel Synagogue, Washington, D.C.; Rabbi Joshua O. Haberman, Rabbi Emeritus, Washington Hebrew

Congregation, Washington, D.C.; Rabbi Robert A. Jacobs, Temple Adas Shalom, Havre de Grace, Maryland; Professor Shlomo Maital, Academic Director of TIM–Technion Institute of Management, Haifa, Israel; Rabbi Isaac Mann, faculty, Academy for Jewish Religion, New York; Rabbi Jonathan A. Schnitzer, z"l, B'nai Israel Congregation, Rockville, Maryland; Rabbi Jeshaia Schnitzer, Rabbi Emeritus, Shomrei Emunah, Montclair, New Jersey; Rabbi Matthew H. Simon, Rabbi Emeritus, B'nai Israel Congregation, Rockville, Maryland; and Rabbi Ira Youdovin, Executive Vice President, Chicago Board of Rabbis.

I am especially grateful to my students whose intelligent and sensitive questions have taught me so much about this faith that we treasure. Their devotion and insight continue to inspire and amaze me.

Finally, to my soulmate and coauthor, Sherie Silverman, whose intellectual companionship and wisdom gave me the courage to persevere—I could not have written this book without you.

$\mathcal{F}$OREWORD

I have had the privilege of knowing Rabbi Bernice K. Weiss for over twenty years. I have watched her evolve from a successful businesswoman with a strong Jewish identity into someone with a budding interest in the rabbinate, followed her sacrificial steps to obtain her rabbinical degree, and then admired the critically important niche she has created in helping non-Jews who are preparing to marry or are already married to Jews develop an appreciation of Judaism and, hopefully, sufficient Jewish identity to convert.

At a time of rampant assimilation and intermarriage, in which more than one in every two Jews who marry do so to a non-Jewish partner, and with conversion rates to Judaism for the non-Jewish the distinct exception, Rabbi Weiss's work is of critical importance to the continuity of Judaism.

She has been remarkably successful because she does not demand conversion as an initial obligation of participating in her program, but rather permits the non-Jewish partner to naturally come to an appreciation and love for the Jewish heritage and religion. By not pushing or pressuring the non-Jewish spouse into conversion, she allows the beauty of the religion to speak for itself. If and when they are ready to convert, she then refers them to another rabbi who performs the actual conversion. But her teaching is so respected that other rabbis readily do so because her students are so well-prepared.

This book is a case study of the remarkable variety of instances she has personally experienced in which non-Jews become Jews. It is thus an inspiration not only for those non-Jews seeking to learn about Judaism, but for Jews who will find their own faith strengthened and reinvigorated. Stories like those of Elizabeth (chapter 11) demonstrate the attraction Judaism provides to those seeking a service of community and spirituality in their lives and the attraction of the Jewish imperative of *tikkun olam*, repairing the world.

There are a number of common threads to these varied, disparate and compelling situations. First, typically the Jewish partners cared enough about their Judaism to encourage their non-Jewish partners to at least examine their religion and understand it. If the Jewish partner takes his or her religion lightly, there is usually no hope the non-Jewish person will ever take the first step to exploring Judaism. Unfortunately, Rabbi Weiss sees only the minority of instances, those in which the Jewish spouse cares enough to transmit his or her interest to his or her fiancé or spouse.

Second, this vital book is candid in making clear that conversion is an initial struggle that imposes strains not only on the couple, but also on each of their families. "Arthur and Janet's Struggle" (chapter 3) vividly portrays the difficulty Janet, the Jewish partner, felt upon entering Arthur's Christian family in Oregon, and the pull of her own family and their religious beliefs on her. "Meredith's Dilemma" (chapter 9) likewise underlines the painful difficulty of leaving Christianity for someone raised in that tradition. This is important for Jews to understand before they seriously entertain marrying a non-Jewish partner—as well as for the non-Jewish partner to contemplate.

Third, these compelling stories underscore the statistical evidence that when there is a conversion to Judaism, the couple tends to be even more Jewishly identified than in many Jewish–Jewish marriages. To break with established religious ties and make the leap of faith to Judaism, the motivation for conversion must be so strong that the convert often intensifies the Jewish identity of the Jewish partner, who may have taken his or her Judaism for granted. The convert gains a real-time, intense understanding of the richness and beauty of the Jewish religion, which can help the Jewish partner rekindle an enthusiasm for Judaism that may have grown cool. This is beautifully portrayed in "Ellen and Joshua's Remarkable Metamorphosis" (chapter 5), in which both spouses become more observant as a result of the other's conversion. Ellen, a Christian from an Asian-American family, brings Joshua to a higher level of Jewish involvement than he had observed before meeting her.

This is also underscored in "Laura's Insatiable Quest" (chapter 6), in which Laura came initially to learn about Judaism rather than to convert, and then developed a love for Judaism that, in turn, helped Adam become more involved in his Judaism.

Fourth, these cases demonstrate that Rabbi Weiss is most successful when the Jewish and non-Jewish partners study with her together. This affords a more loving and supportive environment for the non-Jewish spouse during a difficult and traumatic period. But it is also important to reinforce in the Jewish spouse the importance of Judaism in daily life and in reeducating the Jewish partner to the religious practices, traditions and ethical principles of Judaism. This is portrayed admirably in "Peter and Danielle's Gift" (chapter 7).

Fifth, each of these examples, most particularly "Ezra's Rebirth" (chapter 10), demonstrates Rabbi Weiss's tremendous ability to impart to her students a love for Judaism. Her infectious warmth toward people and reverence for Judaism is crucial to her success.

Her concluding chapter is a short history of Jewish views on conversion. She makes it clear that Judaism, unlike a proselytizing religion, has had mixed views on conversion over its thousands of years of history. But we can no longer afford to be ambivalent about conversion. Intermarriage rates are too high, the threat to Jewish continuity too great, to permit an equivocal response. Rabbi Weiss's example should encourage rabbis and other leaders in the Jewish community—and equally, if not more importantly, parents of Jewish children considering marriage to non-Jews—to proudly encourage an understanding of Judaism and conversion as a positive necessity. And congregations and the Jewish community as a whole must embrace converts without qualification as full and equal members of the Jewish community. Indeed, converts to the faith often can teach those born Jewish about what Judaism really means.

—The Honorable Stuart E. Eizenstat
Deputy Secretary of the United States Department of
the Treasury, Washington, D.C.

Sometimes it's not just by chance that things happen. Some converts have found themselves drawn to Jewish people over the years, and not just to a Jewish boyfriend or girlfriend. It might be a roommate, a teacher, a friend, or even a character in the Hebrew Bible who has touched a responsive chord. Bonds form that eventually lead them to the rabbi's study.

There exists a mystical tradition within Judaism that Jewish souls adrift find their way back to the Jewish people. Could this be the case? You, dear reader, be the judge.

—Rabbi Bernice K. Weiss

*P*REFACE

It's not an easy task to teach my students. These young people come from religious backgrounds where heavy dogma exists. Many were always told what to do, when to pray, sometimes needing someone to pray on their behalf. Now I must open the door to questioning. Judaism is logical. I encourage them to challenge me, to seek explanations that make sense to them.

And I, in turn, am always asking them questions, such as: How can you relate to this God of ours in the year 2000? What does it mean to be a Jew in a world where we are a tiny minority? How can you take the Sabbath and enhance the relationship you have with your Jewish partner? How can you enrich your life with Judaism, yet not take away from the love and respect due your family of birth? That's what appeals to them about Judaism; they like the thinking process. It relieves them of the emotional pressure of inflexibility and nonquestioning.

I nurture my students; I embrace each one of them. When they first come to me, most have no interest in converting; they merely come to learn. I have no vested interest in their converting. However, if they choose it (almost all do), I will arrange it for them. Some will go through more traditional conversions, others, less.

The Hebrew Bible is our text. My students see for themselves where the laws of death and mourning are written, as well as the laws of Shabbat and of keeping kosher; our major holidays are explained in detail. Many of our blessings used in the synagogue originate there. A student who questions will all of a sudden understand why we do the things we do, as with, for example, the laws of circumcision.

Together we hear speakers from the community and visit various synagogues; we study Jewish ethics, Jewish history and the land of Israel. I show them what Shabbat is like, or what Havdallah is like (the ceremony that ends the Sabbath) by sharing it with them in my own home. I hold a kosher cooking class to teach them what it's like to cook in a kosher kitchen.

I love this faith, this heritage, this history, and I feel passionate about introducing it to others. Very often I hear from born Jews that they went to Hebrew school and learned nothing, or that services only bore them. I feel sad that so many are missing so much. Education is the key. Some of my most thrilling moments as a teacher occur when the Jewish partners of my non-Jewish students suddenly throw themselves into Jewish study.

I was lucky to have parents who gave me the gift of Judaism; there were always people in my home celebrating holidays with warmth and togetherness. My father's expertise in Jewish learning defined the way he lived his life. Yet he wasn't judgmental—he never criticized someone who was less or more observant than he. He is the model for how I try to teach.

My students are often appalled by their study of Jewish history. Much of it is terrible, painful to digest, especially the Holocaust. But Judaism is not about suffering; it's about surviving with your values intact. It's not about dying; it's about living in a community, with dignity and holiness. Judaism adds such a dimension to life, such beauty and meaning; it ties us to both the living and the dead, to the past and to the future. I cannot imagine a life without it.

ONE

Introduction

It's by chance, *they say*, that they meet and fall in love. They simply don't think about religion. It's not really surprising, then, that more than half of marriages involving American Jews today are intermarriages. The taboos against religious interdating and intermarriage, for many Jews and non-Jews alike, have largely fallen away. Very often Jewish parents tell me that whether they approve of it or not, they expect their children will marry non-Jews. At the same time, I have had non-Jewish students tell me that it is even "in" to marry Jews. The notion that Jewish men and women make good husbands and wives, that they are good family people, still persists.

Often young Jews who know little about their heritage don't recognize its importance to them until they are confronted with the prospect of marrying a non-Jew. Sometimes those who lacked a Jewish upbringing altogether miss it the most. All of a sudden, they want their children to be Jewish and to live Jewish lives, so they encourage their non-Jewish mates to investigate Judaism.

As a rabbi and teacher, I have taught hundreds of non-Jewish students over the past six years, both in the classroom and in private lessons in the Washington Institute for Conversion and Study of Judaism. When they come to see me, almost all are engaged or married to Jews. A few others have some kind of connection to the Jewish people. (It might be a grandparent or distant relative of Jewish descent.) Generally, these soon-to-be converts—also known as Jews by Choice—are inquisitive, curious individuals who pursue a new way of answering the questions: Who am I? What is the meaning of my life? They are seeking rootedness, warmth and a sense of belonging to a larger family, a community, a people.

At first someone coming into Judaism may feel lost and confused, looking at Judaism from the outside like a child staring at the glittering display window of a toy store. Judaism's four branches—Orthodox, Conservative, Reform and Reconstructionist—offer a variety of avenues of observance, some more readily adaptable than others. The student of Judaism desperately wishes to join an environment that is safe and inviting, and to be welcomed and embraced.

It is my task as their teacher to expose my students to Judaism, but I am unable to give anyone faith. They find faith for themselves. It is a process that defies measurement. Some people need more time, others less. They study Jewish texts; they probe the laws and begin to practice the traditions. Through questioning and examining the consequences of their own actions, they come to believe in something more powerful than themselves, something stronger than anything they can imagine—and they want to feel accountable to that Supreme Being.

But it would be very hard for a convert to reach this point alone; a teacher—a friend or a mentor of sorts—is needed to challenge, stimulate and encourage. I am constantly asked by my students why Jews observe certain rituals and laws—for example, why it is important to observe the Sabbath or place a mezuzah on the door. If a practice makes sense to them, it can add meaning and cohesiveness to their lives. If they learn the reasons behind the traditions of the Jewish wedding, for example, they may want a Jewish ceremony for themselves. Or they may think, *I can keep kosher; it gives me a feeling of belonging.*

Often Jews by Choice assume a much more

devoted approach to Judaism than their born-Jewish spouses, who may be much less knowledgeable of Jewish traditions or who may take Judaism for granted. Converts' enthusiasm for Judaism challenges born Jews to reconsider and, in fact, deepen their commitment to Judaism. Jews by Choice can invigorate a generation that was largely lost to ignorance of its heritage. At a time when the great majority of intermarriages translates into assimilation and a loss for Judaism, and when the number of Jews is so sadly diminished as a result of the Holocaust and low Jewish birth rates, I celebrate the fact that all but a handful of my students have entered into the family of the Jewish people. Along the way, they wrestle with guilt, doubt and fear. As the rabbi who has mentored them personally, week after week, month after month, for about a year's time, I have seen their turmoil, their conflicts, their tears. Some worry that lightning will strike if they decide to convert to Judaism. But they find that instead of *lightning* striking them dead, there's a *lightening* of the soul, a captivation of the heart. As they make their journeys into Judaism, they long to read personal stories of people like themselves, told in their own words. Yet present-day sources that they can turn to for insight and guidance, and to know that they are not alone, are hard to come by. That was the genesis of this book.

I was overwhelmed when so many of my students asked to be included in this volume. Many have remarkable, even powerful, stories to relate. I tried to select stories that would reflect a broad cross-section of experience.

My students are going through an evolution, a transformation that they themselves and, I believe, with God's help are bringing about. They are like Abraham and Sarah, leaving the comfort of the known, the religions of their parents and their youth, to set out on new territory. Birth is traumatic; it takes courage to be reborn. They may miss, even long for, the comfort of the familiar; they may feel guilty for leaving it behind, but, like Abraham and Sarah, they find the struggle worthwhile.

I am in awe of the magnificent new Jews whose spiritual journeys appear on these pages. Names and certain identifying details have been changed to protect their privacy, but with the help of a journalist friend, Sherie Silverman, I have recorded their words as faithfully as possible. They add positive energy to the Jewish people, to be rekindled by future generations. It was a gift to me that they shared their lives with me.

TWO

When You Try
to Please the One You Love

Sharon Explores a New Faith

A striking couple entered my office, referred to me by the rabbi of a major synagogue. Sharon and Seth both had tremendous charisma, sophistication and class. Both were remarkably bright and articulate. Although she had just moved from Belgium, Sharon's English was excellent. However, Seth did most of the talking, explaining that he wanted Sharon to study with me and learn about his Jewish background. My impression was that because she had been brought up in a convent in a European country, with very limited exposure to Jews, Sharon would have a longer journey to Judaism than many of my other students. This is going to be some task, *I thought to myself.*

At her request, I met with Sharon much more frequently than with other students. Yet many of our

7

sessions *didn't deal with the academics at all, but rather with how she could conceivably live a Jewish life. Alone in America, without her family and friends, she was missing the comfort of the known—in her case, Catholicism. She wasn't a reluctant student, but I wasn't sure that studying Judaism was something she really wanted to do. And I wasn't about to push her, because our tradition holds that one should not con- vert for someone else—despite the fact that having a Jewish partner is often the motivating force behind the exploration of Judaism.*

As we progressed through the months, I sensed a continuing resistance on her part, perhaps because Seth was very busy with his work (medical research) and didn't find time to come to the sessions. She felt that studying about Judaism wasn't really the shared experience she had anticipated and was really quite upset that he didn't accompany her. So determined was she to bring him that she picked him up from the airport very early one morning and brought him to a 7:30 A.M. class. I'll never forget that session; Seth was so overwhelmed by what we were studying that he had tears in his eyes. Since then, his attitude about partici- pating with Sharon has been entirely different. He has become her partner in study. As a result, Sharon's attitude has changed as well, and she has embraced

Judaism wholeheartedly. I told Seth to take Sharon to Israel because I sensed that there, Judaism would become a part of her being. As fate would have it, a trip to Israel came up through Seth's work, and he took Sharon along.

Seth Speaks First

I didn't ask Sharon to convert to Judaism or make it a mandatory part of our relationship. I waited, the way you wait for the tulips. Maybe I planted the seed, the bulb. But I never asked her; it would have been too much to ask too quickly. But as our love grew stronger, Sharon just knew. It's for our future together as a family that we share the same values, the values of Judaism.

That's where religion adds synergy and closeness. Some people start with the same religion and build with other things. We started with other things in common and are building with religion. Sharon received her education from Catholic nuns, but we probably wouldn't have fallen in love if she had been the typical convent girl. She had an unusual and very difficult family life, and she wants something different from that in the future. We share a vision of what our family life will be like together. At some point, at a different phase in our lives from where we are now, we will be more organized, more open to having a Jewish home. But it would be wrong to wait for that time without acquiring a knowledge of the fundamentals of Judaism; there's a lot of reward in the transference of knowledge and values. What helps Judaism flourish, what makes it so attractive, is that you have the ability to question and review multiple explanations and interpretations.

Sharon Speaks

I grew up in a Catholic boarding school, praying at lunch, dinner and breakfast, and attending church a minimum of once a day. I wasn't raised by my parents, but by nuns and monks. When we went to bed, we had to cross our hands over our chests, lest God see our breasts. Sometimes I still go to sleep like that. I did not feel compelled to go to mass or confession, but I did pray a lot. Oh, I'm still praying, only now to a different God. My feelings have evolved in such a way that God has become different. In the past, whenever I had a problem or felt sad or really nervous, I always went to church and sat there. It made me really relaxed. I feel I can't do that anymore, and that was difficult to accept for some time.

Yet my Catholicism had been mostly based on God, not Mary or Jesus, and I always had more liking for the Old, rather than the New, Testament; so in that sense I can say to Seth, "My God is also your God." That way I don't feel I betray my old faith in God.

The people I went to boarding school with seemed so superficial—into cars and parties. So I didn't want to go on with them to the Catholic university, even though it was considered the more Catholic, the better. As for me, I had had enough. You make your choices in life. I then had seven years at the non-Catholic university, earning my main degrees in Germanic philology, business communication and international negotiations. I have a master's degree and started my doctorate as well. My higher education made me open-minded, and my job at a postgraduate institute of European studies, where I worked with thirty different nationalities, opened my mind enormously.

Through work I met Seth. He came to Brussels, where we coauthored a book on an infectious disease. A medical doctor, Seth works on health-policy issues and is also a university professor. Although I had read a few books on Judaism before meeting Seth, my only previous Jewish contact was with a girl in boarding school who was part Jewish but did not practice Judaism. After two years of transatlantic dating, I chose to follow Seth to America. But it wasn't an easy decision. I had a very good job in Belgium and my friends around me and my family, so I had to give all that up. In Washington, D.C., I got a job as an official in the economic division of an embassy. In my former job, I was an executive, so I was used to ordering people about. But now people are ordering me about, so career-wise I've taken a step backwards.

Of course, I knew Seth was Jewish, and I quickly came to realize during one of the holidays that Judaism is not only a religion, but also a culture. I felt Seth would not have objected had I not been willing to convert to Judaism, but I felt he wouldn't have been 100 percent at peace either.

Seth was reluctant to speak about being Jewish. I have the impression that many Jewish people are hesitant to admit being Jewish. We Belgians all know Antwerp, with its Hasidim in sidelocks, and the Jews in the antiques market in Brussels. In my language we say, "He is as stingy as a Jew"—a lot of people use this expression—or as wealthy as a Jew. The word

Juif, for Jew, is harsh-sounding. Yet my parents were never anti-Semitic—or against any minorities for that matter. I never heard them utter a word against any other religion. But I do realize that going through conversion to Judaism makes me part of a persecuted group. When I was teaching in Warsaw, I decided to drive out and see Birkenau and Auschwitz. It was horrifying, because when you're actually standing at that place, you can vividly imagine how it must have been. Hopefully, it will never happen again, but one never knows. I'm not hiding my Judaism or the least bit afraid of showing it. I wear the Jewish Chai symbol around my neck, and already at the embassy where I work they are assigning me files on Jewish matters.

At first my mother didn't say anything when I told her Seth was Jewish. Then she said, "It doesn't really matter what he is as long as he takes care of you." It so happens that she loves Seth. With my father, a retired human-resources director, it was more difficult. The Jewish religion he is not really bothered about, but he refused to meet Seth because he disapproves of my choice of an American who doesn't even speak our language.

My grandmother on my mother's side is a descendant of a French aristocratic family; one ancestor was chancellor of the exchequer in the seventeenth century. We had a couple of castles, and my grand-mother still owns some real estate in France. My father is a farmer's son who eloped with my mother, with the result that her parents did not speak to her for a couple of years, until I was born in fact. My grandmother always said, "There will always be a division between the aristocracy and the others."

Because he was an outsider, my father more than anything wanted me to marry an aristocrat. It would provide him the perfect opportunity to raise himself through me. In fact, that was the direction my life had been taking before I met Seth. I had been engaged to a well-known baron whom I knew from school, but whom I regarded more as a brother or friend. I have always had a strong sense of responsibility toward my family, and I had this feeling of duty toward my father. He is a very domineering person; I was scared of my father really. It has only been a couple of years since I got out of this proposed marriage to the baron. The pressure on me from my father was enormous; now he can't show off to anyone.

I knew my parents had an unhappy marriage—I have no recollection whatsoever of their exchanging affection. My mother was terrified of my father. He abused her physically. And if you see that as a child, you see it the rest of your life. He would drop her off, just push her out of the car, in the middle of the night somewhere. Somehow she managed to come back home. I have a lot of painful memories like that. It was easier for me when I was far away from home and not confronted with it. But bit by bit, I learned to loosen myself from my father's grip—though he tries to this very day to put some kind of guilt trip on me. Of course, I also love my father from the emotional point of view. You can't turn your back on your own flesh and blood. And he is beginning to accept the idea of my marrying Seth. When he saw me recently, he realized that I'm happy with my life now. He said, "Well, you look very good." In his own way he loves me.

For twenty years my father actually led a double life. Three days a week he spent with my mother, and four days a week with a younger male friend. I always thought he was away on business. I never imagined that he was having an affair. My mother knew about it from the beginning, but divorce wasn't acceptable. She never told anyone about it until I was twenty-one or twenty-two. My childhood and youth were not easy. My mother was sick with throat cancer and suffered from severe depression as well. For me, being able to go through all of that, just knowing that I was able to survive, makes me think I'm capable of handling almost anything.

Children who come from situations like mine can go two ways: Reproduce the life you have or figure out for yourself what you would like to identify with and find it. I can say I never will be with a man who hits me or cheats on me because I have taken lessons out of my past. I don't want a loveless relationship like my parents had; I want a loving relationship. I look forward to creating a home and sharing a family life with Seth. My mother never cooked or cleaned, but I like to do domestic things. I know what it is like not to have a home life. Even on Christmas we were not together. My father was always out; my mother was always depressed. Sometimes I say, "I've got parents, but no home to go back to." That is hard to acknowledge. My friends have become my family. For me, home is my friends, even if those friends have families of their own. Fortunately, I had a nanny who was very loving, a warm, outstanding woman who died when I was ten. Her name was Rachel. Along with my school, she had a positive influence on me. To this day, I feel her as very much a presence in my life, and if ever I have a daughter, I'll call her Rachel. I fell in love with Seth, but not blindly. Until my mother became ill, I never had a really close relationship with either of my parents, so I'm still trying to get used to Seth's closeness with his family. I haven't quite figured out the closeness of Jewish families.

With regard to accepting Judaism, going to Israel with Seth this year definitely changed me. There was this shock, seeing the clash between Judaism and Christianity in Israel. It was a little weird for me. The religion of my youth was so deeply rooted. Until I was twenty-five or twenty-six, I had gone to church every week. But seeing the monks in their robes moved me to be confronted with the realization that Catholicism was now only a tradition for me, no longer a religion I practiced. It was a reaffirmation for me that what Catholicism stands for is not really what I stand for. It made me realize there's no turning back. And I don't want to turn back. I'm at ease with myself. It was actually a good test for me.

At the Western Wall, it was very emotional for me to see people praying so fervently. For Seth, too, it was highly emotional. There's a small place there for women. I was praying and writing my wishes on paper, and tucking the paper into the wall. And then Seth took out a prayer from one of the books that Rabbi Weiss had given him. It was about two people starting a new life together. So then he said, "This is the place where I became a man and this is the place where I would like to become a husband." Before I knew it, he was down on his knees and proposing to me. I was just crying and crying. At first I didn't answer, I was so overwhelmed. I expected we would get married at some point; it was the logical conclusion. But I did not expect to become engaged like that, in such a romantic fashion (he had carried the prayer in his wallet all the way from home). My conversion to Judaism some time later was special, but it wasn't the powerfully present experience the Israel trip was. It was more the normal result of the trip, more a formality. The transformation had already taken place.

When Sharon and Seth came back from Israel, Sharon had an engagement ring on her finger, a blue sapphire with white diamonds around it, to represent Israel's colors, blue and white. They came to see me together, both full of energy and life. I never before had sensed such excitement in either of them. Sharon told me about how Seth had become so emotional in Israel that he got down on his hands and knees near the Western Wall and asked her to marry him. This was where he had become a Bar Mitzvah at age thirteen (he is now thirty-five), and where he wanted to propose to his wife-to-be in order to carry on the heritage of his grandparents to future generations. Later, they traveled around Israel, visiting the ruins and walking in the Old City of Jerusalem. Sharon told me how she knew at last that she had come home. Her conflicts about what it means to embrace Judaism and raise a Jewish family faded. She recognized that among the Jewish people is where she belongs.

THREE

When You're Afraid to Tell Your Parents

Arthur and Janet's Struggle

Arthur had no problem introducing Janet, who is Jewish, to his parents, but he was, and still is, very fearful of telling them that he is converting to Judaism. By abandoning the faith of his youth, he may feel like he is turning his back on them. He is concerned that they might not understand, that they might be hurt or angry. Arthur has always been close to his family, so perhaps he can't bear to create a barrier that could separate them.

When he tried to explain to his parents and brothers his commitment to Judaism, he felt it didn't really penetrate. He probably didn't tell them as fully, as completely, as was needed. Maybe there is a little guilt on his part, or, in his words, a feeling of "not wanting to rock the boat."

Arthur and Janet come from quite different

backgrounds: He grew up on a farm in an isolated area of Oregon; she was the daughter of a doctor and always lived near a big city. They met at Cornell University, where he was a graduate student and she was an undergraduate. Arthur said he'd had girlfriends before, but meeting Janet was different from anything he had experienced. He used to think that those who say you just know when the right person comes along were off base. But after knowing Janet for a mere week, he changed his mind.

At first Janet was afraid to tell her parents that she was in love with Arthur. Her family was not religiously observant, but she knew how important it was to them that she marry within the Jewish faith. For over a year she kept their relationship a secret.

Then Arthur, who once taught in a Christian Sunday school, and Janet, who never went to religious school and knew very little about her heritage, suddenly decided it was important for both of them to explore Judaism together. It is a joy to teach them both; I have not seen a couple in a long time that so easily exchanges ideas as the two of them. Before they had started to study, Arthur told me, at night they would just watch TV. Now they look forward to reading books and picking topics of interest within the context of Judaism. They never miss a class and attend each seminar, bringing fresh questions every week. They have begun to observe Shabbat and attend synagogue, and soon they will have a Jewish wedding.

In a gentle and loving way, Arthur gradually will have to expose his family to the tradition he now calls his own. My guess is he will be surprised to see that they accept and respect his choice of a new way of life when they are assured that their place in his heart has not been undermined.

Arthur's Spiritual Journey

I grew up outside a small town in Oregon on thirty-five acres of forest land, where my parents planted and sold Christmas trees. The nearest neighbor was a half mile away, and it was a considerable trip to town. There was little diversity in our town: In fact, it was about as small-town WASP American as you can get. Not that there was anything much to the town then. There are four stoplights now and a Wal-Mart, so I guess today it's a real center of culture!

When my dad was laid off from his job as a laborer in a sawmill during my senior year of high school, I was nervous about how I would be able to afford college at the University of Oregon. I had saved some money working on farms from the age of fourteen, and my parents tried to help me fill in the gaps. (My mother is a secretary and my father continues to work as a painter and carpenter.)

Farmwork actually started for me at age ten, with strawberry picking. I was saving up money for bell-bottom pants—thirty-five dollars a pair compared to straight legs from Sears at ten dollars a pair. I finally earned enough to buy them, but that was the year straight legs came back, so I was stuck with two pairs. I was just a nerdy kid.

My parents taught us the hard-work ethic. Most weekends every fall were spent hauling and splitting wood, because our house was heated by a wood-burning stove. It was a very Oregon kind of thing, or at least it used to be. I'm the first one in my family to go to college and get a degree and the only one to go to graduate school. My high school class started out with 220, but by graduation 70 had dropped out. A number of girls got pregnant and quit. Maybe twenty or thirty of my classmates went on to some kind of college; most of the others went into the military. I have an older brother in the National Guard and a younger brother who is a full-time carpenter. We grew up very close because we were in the middle of nowhere and we spent our summers together. Even though our paths have diverged—we're about as different as we can be—because of that fundamental base, we remain very close. Whenever we get together, we stay up all night chatting.

My dad barely passed high school, but he is very interested in current events, very engaged. While our town was extremely homophobic and quite racist, my parents—though not exposed to book learning—were intuitively open-minded and intellectually curious. If I had half the common sense my father has, I would go a lot further in life. My parents imparted to me a tremendous curiosity about the world.

My mother had been raised a Lutheran, but neither of my parents was interested in religion or attending church. They believed in God but were disillusioned by what they felt was the hypocrisy of religious institutions and the people who paraded themselves as godly. However, my grandmother took my brothers and me every Sunday to a Lutheran Sunday school. While my brothers lost interest and didn't continue after age ten or twelve, I went on to be confirmed. I remember stirring things up with the confirmation class because I couldn't understand how evolution fit in with the Bible. Even so, I became a Sunday school teacher for the fourth grade when I was a senior in high school.

I've always felt very drawn to exploring the spiritual side of things. I suppose I'm a weird mix of a lot of things. I've always been complicated—the strange brother, the oddball middle child who read encyclopedias in the summer because I was bored. A straight-A student in high school, I was embarrassed by being a nerd; to try to undo the nerdiness, I spent a great deal of time partying on Saturday nights. I just wanted to fit in.

My spiritual journey led me from a small town to a hippie college town (Eugene), to a small town in Central America (during my junior year of college), to a graduate program at an Ivy League school, to a job as a government policy wonk (work only, no kids) in Washington, D.C. In college I sometimes attended Friends (Quakers) meetings. Then came Nicaragua, where I worked in a war-refugee housing project. That immersion in international justice and environmental issues—that's where I got more in touch with God. God became more real to me, and my life changed forever. It made me realize all the gifts you're blessed with. Right and wrong were simpler, more clear-cut. The struggle to survive was paramount. The struggle for me was to let go of my judgmentalism. I know that being in Central America at that time made me a better person.

Regarding Christianity, I always had this conundrum of the righteous man in some remote spot like the mountains of Papua, New Guinea. The Christian doctrine that gave me the most trouble was that you had to believe in Jesus Christ in order to be saved—that was my understanding—and all those righteous people in New Guinea or wherever who didn't believe in Jesus would perish. This conundrum I could never figure out to my satisfaction. I did a lot of reading, but none of the answers were satisfying. It struck me that a just God wouldn't think that way; it was a fundamental contradiction to me. The point should be to live your life in a godly way, live by the commandments.

I became interested in Judaism in college. My first exposure was through my boss when I was a hall resident. He would tell me about his family's Jewish traditions and rituals, and I was really curious about it. Later, when I met Janet, I learned how important Judaism is to her. I had never experienced the cultural part of it—the whole idea of the holidays, the celebrations, the history and of being part of a minority. There is the knee-jerk reaction to being part of the Chosen People. Some feel threatened by the concept: I guess it's a combination of blessing and burden. But being a Jew can't be all peaches and cream. A kid of mine may come home one day crying because he is not accepted. Maybe this is something I haven't fully appreciated yet. But you take the pebbles with the milk and honey.

Janet and I talked about taking courses in Judaism for a long time. If I was to be part of her family, I wanted to learn more about their Jewish heritage. We have been together two and a half years, but the watershed event for me was the first night of Passover at Janet's aunt and uncle's house. I felt completely welcomed and that the family was happy about my being there. There was no pressure to become something I was not—I wouldn't have responded well to that. It was wonderful the way the family itself was the center of the celebration. We asked during the seder, What does this Passover mean to you? To me, then, this felt like everything religion should be about: community, family togetherness, remembering the importance of what the Passover event marks, reminding everybody through stories and traditions and even goofy little games. For the first time, I was able to understand why Judaism is so important to Janet. It definitely touched me spiritually to remember what it means to come out of terrible conditions, to be a part of a people, and to do the things, the rituals, that connect you across space and history.

As I was coming closer to Judaism, I had to confront those hidden things, emotional chords, that remained from my early practice of Christianity. I wondered, *If I say I'm a Jew, does that mean I have to say I reject Jesus?* That triggered a guilt mechanism. I had always been discontent with the Christian idea of the inherently sinful nature of man. But even though I said I was beyond that, there was still that little fear that asked, *What are you doing rejecting Jesus? How can you have been one thing and then be something else?* I had to come to terms with my core guilt. Intellectually I was ready to become a Jew, but emotionally, it took more time. You can't become Jewish overnight. You feel things in your heart; you feel when it is right for you.

I knew in my heart that I wanted to get past the guilt. I had a vision of what would fulfill me, a vision Janet and I shared. A practicing Jew—that's the kind of person I wanted to be, focusing on performing the mitzvahs (commandments), and leading a family-centered life. I've been lucky enough to have had this evolution, this direction where I have always been headed. Now a tremendous new world has opened for me, a world I knew little about before dating Janet.

I have always believed very strongly in the presence of God. The universe reflects a constant struggle between order and chaos, yet it holds together and makes sense. Judaism says your mission in life is to do your best while you are here on earth; it's what you do with your existence that counts. Judaism challenges us to do more than follow a set of rules. Ultimately it is up to us to choose our own path to righteousness.

Janet: Entering "Another Universe"

I knew it meant a lot to my family for me to marry someone who is Jewish; it had been said to me. So for an entire year I couldn't tell my parents about Arthur even though I was two years out of college and spending every moment I could with him. It was very stressful because I'm very close to my parents.

Yet they didn't belong to a synagogue, and I had never had a Bat Mitzvah. Rather than religious observance, Judaism was something built into me, involving every aspect of my life—the family, going to visit my grandmother in New York, the foods we eat, the conversations we have.

In college I attended Jewish-studies courses and

began dating Jewish men. I had a certain feeling about non-Jewish men: Don't shop where you can't buy. There was the kids issue: Don't you want to raise your kids Jewish? Don't you want to transmit to them what you have? I had painted a picture for myself of a marriage like my older sister's. I wanted a nice Jewish boy; that was my picture. So when Arthur and I grew increasingly committed to one another, I was painfully conflicted. Meanwhile, my parents were setting me up on dates. I just blew them off, and my parents thought . . . who knows what? Maybe that I was a lesbian, because for a year and a half I kept turning down these dates. During this time I introduced Arthur to my parents, almost eased him into the family, as just a friend.

Finally, I asked my father, "Dad, aren't you wondering if I'm dating Arthur?" His initial reaction was that he was very happy for me because Arthur had received rave reviews from them; but the first question out of my mother's mouth was, "Is he going to convert?" I told her that we were not there yet. The way they got to know Arthur first as a friend was a good strategy. Instead of being Arthur the guy who's not Jewish, he was Arthur. They saw that we were very happy together. If Arthur didn't convert to Judaism, they would still be supportive and happy for us.

Arthur and I did talk about the possibility of his converting to Judaism, however. It was important to me that he understand what Judaism meant to me, and that I would hope he would convert or want to participate in whatever traditions I would incorporate in my life. I wanted to learn a lot more about the traditions, and I knew I wanted my children to be exposed to them. I did not say to Arthur, and I still have not said, that he should convert. He would not accept that. That is not what our relationship is built on. But he has known from day one that I plan to raise my kids as Jewish kids. After our first date, he mentioned he would be pleased to attend a Passover seder. He was interested, and I thought to myself, that's a good sign. With the few non-Jewish men I had dated, I had hesitated to talk about being Jewish until later in the relationship, but with Arthur, I talked about it right away. It was right there; I needed him to understand that about me.

I had expected Arthur to feel strange at my parents' house, to feel overwhelmed, because it is so unlike home life in a small town. I expected some reaction from him. Yet he was totally unfazed. But going with Arthur to meet his family in Oregon was an adventure. We took a one-lane gravel road with all kinds of twists and turns—every member of the family has hit a deer on it—and I entered another universe.

The first time I walked into Arthur's parents' house, his dad pulled me over to see Arthur's first kill—showed me the antlers on the wall. I had to sleep in a room of animal heads—some were just antlers, but some were full heads: antelope, elk, mule deer (the bear got brittle and had to be taken down last Christmas). The first two days I was there I felt weird: the cowboy hats, the big silver belt buckles, the ham, the pickup truck—I'm not used to all that. There were the cousins who asked me if I had a Christmas tree. There were those moments concerning wedding preparations: Arthur's father asked me twice if we break plates. "No," I said. "We don't do that. That's a Greek thing." I felt a little defensive. One cousin said, "I didn't know you people still existed; I've never even met a Jewish person." I wondered if they were trying to make me feel alien. It was the first time I felt separated from Arthur. I felt nervous. I didn't know how I was going to make it through the rest of the week. Then there was this otherworldly experience of meeting Arthur's grandfather for lunch. He lives in a trailer home, and I had never known anyone in a trailer home, had never even been in one.

But after two days with the family, I felt totally comfortable. His parents had a fireplace where we sat around and talked and talked—and they seemed genuinely interested in me. After two days, I felt like I had Arthur back. It was the same Arthur. We had spent two years isolated from our families, having just each other. I had just needed some time to digest being with his family.

Recently a perplexing dilemma presented itself: Arthur's brother had just had a baby and wanted Arthur to be the child's godfather. That meant if something should happen to the parents, Arthur and Janet would have to raise the child as a Christian. Arthur was genuinely torn because here he was, becoming a Jew and entering the family of Judaism. He was struggling between two loyalties: his allegiance to his brother on the one hand and his allegiance to a new faith on the other. He thought about it long and hard, and I give him a lot of credit for taking his conversion to Judaism so seriously. See how he handled the first serious family dilemma he would face.

A Family Dilemma

My brother recently e-mailed me to be the sponsor of his child's baptism. My grandmother passed away three years ago, and my brother had the thought that to keep Grandma's memory alive, he would baptize this child at the church where she had been so active over the years. I didn't e-mail him back right away because it struck me that I had a dilemma. I wanted to do this for my family, to be the spiritual godparent to my brother's child. My brother and I respect each other's worldview. But then I realized that I hadn't laid the groundwork sufficiently as to what Janet and I were doing religiously—beyond just taking classes with the rabbi. I was okay with committing to being a spiritual guide or supportive spiritual mentor; I felt it would be a ceremonial thing to support my family, not to support church doctrine. If I didn't participate, there would have been no other way for my family to interpret it than as a slap in the face.

As Rabbi Weiss suggested to me, I met with the pastor ahead of time to run through the program. I said, "I'm not comfortable with that paragraph and my saying 'I do' to that," but I didn't see a way out of it. My family doesn't understand fully where I'm at now, in a religious sense, and that's nobody's fault but my own. I don't think I fully grasped how uncomfortable it would feel for both Janet and me to be there. I realized at that moment that what had been holding me back from conversion to Judaism was my concern about how my family would feel about it. That was the real issue I hadn't dealt with yet.

Janet's Impression

At the baby-naming, Arthur and his family were singing the hymns and songs for the sake of his late grandmother. But to hear those words coming out of Arthur's family members' mouths, words I have been taught to fear, I guess—"Jesus Christ our Savior, our Lord," to be referred to as "the Jews"—it was a bit overwhelming. I realized that by marrying into Arthur's family, this was a part of me now. I felt guilty, like I was betraying my own family.

Arthur's Conclusion

Sitting there in that church reaffirmed for me my lack of comfort with the dogma of the church. It was one of the strongest feelings I had. I realized that since I left home, I had taken a radically different path from my family. My aunt told my dad that Pastor Dave offered to come out to Washington to do the Lutheran part of our wedding. I had to remind Dad that ours will be a strictly Jewish wedding. My parents are very curious about Judaism, and are wondering why it is so important to me that the wedding be Jewish. And they may have a fear that they might not fit in or understand what is going on. I would like to make them feel comfortable, but it may be that my family and I don't have a good basis for dialoguing on serious things. Yet they have always known that I have been on this spiritual journey, and they've been incredibly accepting in the past.

I think this experience in the church made me more committed than ever to Judaism. It forced me to explore this vague, lingering feeling of guilt that is wrapped up with my relationship with my family. It clarified for me where my guilt was coming from; it was not at all a philosophical-religious guilt.

Judaism is the belief system I feel most at home with. I have evolved; I know I'm ready to embrace it. I'm there now and it feels comfortable. It's important to have a set of values that you cannot just embrace and accept, but be challenged by. Judaism has a framework that, unlike any other, allows me to continue growing and developing. And you need tradition for the establishment of your family, to give your children a foundation for spirituality. Wisdom and insight come from having a solid base in something you're grounded to.

But conversion isn't the end of the journey; it's not the end of the process. The evolution has to continue for both Janet and me. I'm a work in progress, and I always want to be. That's what being Jewish means to me.

FOUR

"If You're Jewish, You'll Burn in Hell"

Jill: The Small-Town Girl "Gone Bad"

 *Jill is a beautiful young woman, with long flowing blond hair, an angelic smile and twinkling eyes; Harvard educated and an editor for a major magazine, she's an articulate speaker as well as an attentive listener.*

Someone who comes from an abusive childhood, if they are as intelligent as Jill, will look for a partner who is a nurturer. That's what Jill found in Doug, a bright young man who holds a prestigious government position. She was looking for a relationship that would bring her all the kindness her father never gave her. She also fell in love with Doug's parents. All the tumult of Jill's upbringing has been laid to rest because of her entering Doug's family.

At first Jill was very apprehensive about studying with me. While she and Doug had already agreed that their children would be raised Jewish, she had no interest in conversion to Judaism. When Doug first called, he wanted to make sure I wouldn't push her. Doug was very supportive of Jill; whatever she wanted to do, he kept saying over and over, he would go along with it. Due to her taxing work schedule, Jill could come to study only very early in the morning or late at night. Week after week, she arrived at 7 A.M. or after 8 P.M. Doug accompanied her every single time.

Jill challenged me; she asked me countless questions; she thought through ideas. Her inquisitive mind wanted to better understand Doug's background, so she was studying for his sake—but for herself as well.

Jill never just read the written page: She went beyond. That's what her gift is. You could see her thinking about what it must have been like in biblical or medieval times. She put herself into the situation and thought about how people would have reacted.

Gradually, Jill realized that Judaism fit her. "I never was comfortable in my background," she said to me. "Judaism suits me." At this point, she was converting for herself; she is too smart to let anybody tell her what to do. Jill's a survivor, a very strong personality; she doesn't waver. Once she makes up her mind, she does not turn back.

Jill's Story

I was sixteen, a new driver, and went to pick up my friend Cindy to go to a church bowling party. But Cindy didn't want to go, so she and I went to a movie instead. My parents happened to drive past the church and saw that my vehicle was not there. My mom got really angry because she knew all hell would break loose. When I came home that night my father pushed my head into the ground with such force that my teeth went through my lip. I was swallowing so much blood that I thought I was going to die. I couldn't breathe; blood was everywhere.

My mom told my father to stop. "That's enough, Harvey; for God's sake, that's enough," she said. Then she said to me, "Get as far away from here as fast as you can and don't come back." And that's what I decided to do.

My father is a troubled person. A civil engineer who owns two small foundation companies, he met my mom when they were teenagers. She worked to put my dad through college; now she stays at home. My father's own mom died when he was very little, and his dad wasn't around, so he raised himself. He's volatile and really violent. You never know what's going to set him off. It can be very scary. My dad used to load up his guns and run around the house claiming he was going to kill all of us and then himself. He shoots the gun out the front door or the back window; it still makes the house shake inside. Everyone who knows him knows he's a hothead. You don't cross Harvey.

I was pretty rebellious, I guess, but my dad's such a control freak that he saw any attempt to be a normal person as rebellion. I got spanked once a week. (He was a huge spanker.) He would hit me and my mom. He felt entitled to do it. He was so forceful—he would throw you against the wall before he knew what he had done. "I get angry because other people are screwed up," my dad would say. "There's nothing wrong with me."

My mom has wanted to break up with him since she was fifteen (she's now fifty). But she's been terrorized by him. He'd smash his car into hers; he's threatened to kill her family as well as her. She says she's stayed with him all this time because that's where she's the safest, containing the monster. Otherwise, she'd go off and be in the Peace Corps and change her name.

I was raised in a small town in the Midwest, in an evangelical, conservative German Lutheran church, one step shy of fire and brimstone. It had pictures of fetuses on the wall to shock people. When I was eight years old, three times a week I'd go to church— Wednesday after school, Saturday morning and Sunday morning.

They taught us that if an infant is born and dies before it has been baptized, it goes to hell and spends eternity burning there. That was why it's essential to baptize babies immediately. So here I am in third grade, and I just know that's not how the universe works.

At age eight, when I realized this particular Protestant church was loony, I de facto became an independent spiritual seeker, for lack of a better word. I was a big reader as a kid, one of those nerds, bookworms. My parents are very primitively religious, anti-intellectual; it's a sin to have any doubts; you don't question. I toed the company line and got confirmed, but they knew that I thought the church was wrong about a lot of things.

If I brought up a point that I disagreed with, it would make them nervous. Because the very idea of questioning or disagreeing is bad—almost like having an idol, or any other major sin. There's this thing in Christianity where if you have doubts, the last thing you can do is express them. By age eight, we had it drilled into our heads that there is one unforgivable sin and once you commit it, there's no hope—and that sin is to say that Jesus is not God or that you don't have to believe in Jesus to go to heaven. From the time we could talk and walk, we were taught that you spend eternity in agony if you ever mouth those words. That means I don't know what my own brother thinks religiously (he's eight years younger), because if we have doubts we have them secretly.

I was married before I met Doug—right out of college, to a classmate from Harvard. About three hundred and fifty people attended my first wedding—the whole town, the dentist, the first-grade teacher, etc. It was a Christian Lutheran wedding. My first husband was part Jewish (his father was Jewish; his mother was Episcopalian). While he identified himself as a secular Jew, he did not practice Judaism. Yet he begged the minister not to mention the word Jesus in the ceremony. (The minister may have done that once or twice anyway.)

My marriage was a kind of scandal in my hometown. People are rather prejudiced and anti-Semitic there. They assumed my former husband was Jewish because of his name—there was no subtlety or nuance or distinction made. This small-town girl had gone bad because all knew that if you were Jewish, you'd burn in hell for eternity. That's the public stance. Even though there may be a number of open-minded people, you don't hear any open-minded speech.

I was twenty-three, very deferential to my parents. I thought at the time, They're throwing me the wedding; it's a big wedding; we'll do it their way. There's no doubt I disappointed them, especially my father. My dad even offered me lots of money to elope. He'd probably claim that as a joke now, but I don't think it was.

At the rehearsal dinner my dad announced to whoever could hear him that the wedding was off, and then he vanished. At 4 A.M. the next morning, the morning of my wedding day, he woke me up. "I need to talk to you," he said. It was a command; I was held hostage. So I sat there forever—two hours—till dawn, sat on a screened-in back porch. He said, "Tell me, is it or is it not true that if you don't believe in Jesus you go to hell?"

My mom was there too. She would step in and say, "Harvey, I think that Jesus introduces himself to everyone when you die, so you get a second chance— one last chance—to believe in Jesus before being sent to hell." She would try anything to help the situation along. What he was talking about wasn't really the issue, though. Here's a man with intense emotions that he himself can hardly understand or control. It starts in his body; he's upset and he needs to be placated or calmed down. There's no reasoning with him; it's like trying to settle down a crazy person. He would almost get angrier if we tried to answer his challenge. It was just more frustrating to him. What he really wants to hear is, "You are right." Usually you can take the "you are right" approach with him, but he was trying to say that we should cancel the wedding. There are times when you need to stand your ground. Eventually he wore himself out. Later that day he walked me down the aisle as if nothing had ever happened, with a pink rose and a pink cummerbund to match my mom's dress.

Everybody is still shocked in that town that I married a Jew. To this day, I'm sure they still talk about it. It's the kind of town where people would say to each other that they felt sorry for my parents because of it. My mom's answer was, "I heard that they treat their women very well, that they're very sensitive men." This was her best take on it to others. I remember thinking that it was one of those prejudiced, ignorant statements when the person doesn't realize they're being offensive because they're saying something positive. But I've thought about it ever since. I remember thinking to myself at the time how wonderfully my first husband treated me, but I didn't associate it with Judaism.

There's no cultural ethic to treat your wife well in my town. If I go home and meet the guys I went to school with, they treat me badly; they don't have it in them to be polite or interested in me as a person. As a woman in that town, my only role is to be a trophy or a listener, so they can have a captive audience. I see it as a geographic thing in this little pocket of the country. It's a rugged man's world; it's men who are running the equipment; they are the ones doing the heavy lifting.

My first marriage lasted three years. My first husband was unfaithful and gambled our money away. My dad claims that he knew all along that my first husband and his family were bad people. When I happened to go back to the town dentist a couple of years ago, he asked me how my husband was. I said we got a divorce, and he said, "Oh, because he was Jewish, right?"

I see my father only once a year, at Christmastime, for three or four days; everything's hustle and bustle then. I speak to Mom on the phone once a month. The dynamic is, she gives me the update on everything that's happening in this little world that I left.

We're close, yet we don't have an intimate knowledge of each other's lives. Doug, my new fiancé, and I are planning to move to California after we're married, but my parents don't know that. They know so little about my life in general that it would seem bizarre to tell them.

My father does not learn from his mistakes. When I went home for Christmas this past year—my annual trip—he blew up, exploding and cursing in the restaurant. Not only is he just as bad as ever, but he's unrepentant, unapologetic about it. He's like a bomb; you can't be with him because you never know when he'll explode. I got really scared. Here I am, thirty years old now, and this man has been threatening me and my mom my whole life. We walked outside the restaurant, but I was too afraid to get in the car with him. He drives through ditches and swerves into oncoming traffic; he'll do anything to frighten us. I didn't want to go home either, so I just wandered around in the dark. Then it dawned on me that I had my purse with a ticket in it. I realized I could go back to my life on the East Coast. I walked down to the truck stop on the interstate and stayed there over night. The next morning I left town.

Here's my dilemma: I haven't spoken to my father since that moment in the restaurant. I must decide whether to continue to be a part of my family. I feel bad because my grandparents are on their deathbeds, and I was very close to them. They spoiled me rotten, doted on me a lot; I spent several weeks every summer on their farm. That was heaven. My grandfather was like Jimmy Stewart. Whenever I complained about my dad to him, he said my dad had a very generous heart. It's true he has a good heart; but he has a monster living inside him, and you never know when the monster will take over.

I do feel guilty—not lately, but sometimes—about not being more of a daughter. My parents may not even come to our wedding in a few weeks. (Of course, it's my second wedding.) Both my grandparents have severe heart problems, and my mother is exhausted from taking care of them. Now my dad says he and my mom are not coming to our wedding unless he gets a major apology from me. My mom says she will be there anyway—on her brave days. They don't know I'm going through the conversion process. They should know that Doug is Jewish; I mentioned it, but I didn't make a big deal out of it. That was in the early days when I didn't realize that Doug felt so strongly about having the whole family practice Judaism.

Doug and I talked about religion and how we

would raise our kids before we got engaged last year. At this point, we had already been together three and a half years. This was where we clashed—the religion issue. It was the deciding factor as to whether we should get married. For Doug, it was very important—his Judaism is the main identifying factor in his life. (I've always been a very religious person myself.) I said half a dozen times to Doug, "Why did you ever start dating me, knowing I'm not Jewish?" It seems he had hoped I would convert, but he was afraid to bring it up in the early days of our relationship.

At the magazine where I work, Doug was the cute boy by the elevator. That's how I thought of him before I met him; I wondered who he was. I was shameless and introduced myself. "Welcome to the magazine," I said. "If there's anything you need here, come to me." He said he was thinking at the time, "Why is this beautiful woman talking to me?"

There's something about the Jewish men I've met; from what I've seen they have an added dimension. A lot of guys are lacking a feminine, empathetic, thoughtful side. I row crew with a bunch of guys. There's something missing—a reflective spirituality. The Jewish men that I know make it clear that they're trying to be good people and live good lives and put ideals above self-interest. With Doug, his father, their friends, my impression is that that's the spirit of it. Doug and his dad are both self-effacing. Even though they achieve a lot, they know there's something more important than themselves; they're humble.

"Now, about converting," my future in-laws said to me after dinner the night we announced our engagement. It upset me at the time. Doug had just slipped the ring on my finger a few days before on a surprise trip to Florida. When we got back to town, his parents welcomed us with hugs and kisses. Then it was sort of, "Let's clear the dinner table and have the conversion talk." So I was shocked; I was stunned. I was really turned off.

But they explained that Judaism was the most important thing in their lives. I suppose they felt that my religious identity wasn't their business before (I was just a person their son was dating), but now that I was becoming a part of their family, it was very much their business. It was their family and I was joining it.

I asked them a number of questions (I couldn't think of anything else to do). I had learned a lot because Doug had brought me to Passover seder, and we would celebrate Rosh Hashanah together, and I fasted with him on Yom Kippur. Many Friday evenings we would go for Shabbat dinner at the folks' house, so I had been soaking it all in. I think I didn't understand that there was much to be studied.

As a girl, I had to memorize and recite the Old Testament aloud—one or two chapters at a time—working my way forward every Saturday. I was a big showoff because it was easy for me to memorize. I'd go on and on until they would have to tell me to stop. It was kind of obnoxious, but I liked it. My thought that evening at Doug's parents was that Christianity was Judaism plus Jesus. That meant Judaism was just Christianity minus Jesus. I mistakenly thought I knew Judaism (I knew it better than my first husband—that's for sure).

I was trying to figure out why my converting was so important to Doug and his parents. Was it important religiously or culturally? Did they want me in the fold because this is what God wants us to do—to be Jews and not Christians? Maybe it was more about ancestor worship. They seemed to be saying that being Jewish is not about God, but about being part of a family that has survived against all odds. Doug feels honored and obligated to keep that going. He would say, "I have intense love and respect for my ancestors. I'm grateful to them, and I want to carry on their legacy."

"You mean, you don't really believe that Moses received the Ten Commandments from God?" I asked. In my family, you'd be struck dead by lightning for saying you doubted that. I believe absolutely that Moses must have chiseled those things away; he believed he was in communion with a perfect, divine Source of Truth, and my guess is he was right. At this point, I'd joke to Doug's parents, "I'm more Jewish than you are; I believe that Moses was given the Ten Commandments by God."

My family is so passionate about the idea that Christ is your Lord and Savior that it's a massive blow for me to convert; it's like an earthquake. First, in Christianity it's your duty to save another person's soul; my conversion would be a reflection on my family. The onus is on them to bring me back; otherwise, twice as many people are going to hell. Just imagine your worst personal hell; that's what you get.

My mom gave faith to me, this innocent faith that you wish you could give to everyone. It's never dawned on her for one split second that she's not a child of God. When I was a little kid, I always had these dialogues with Jesus in my head. Jesus champions you, will always be there for you; Jesus is unconditional love. He's a character you adore, who wants the best for you. It's a beautiful image. There is somebody out there who will protect you—especially someone whose dad beats her up.

I basically said to Jesus, "I know you wouldn't send anybody to hell because they didn't believe in you. That doesn't make any sense." So I created my own brand of Christianity. There is no such thing as hell. God would never ever send anyone to hell; the only hell is the hell we make for ourselves. So basically I've had this private religion. If there is a God, my view of Jesus is what I envision God to be—ever forgiving, ever loyal; I believe in a Jesus-like loving God, but not in Christianity. I never felt Jesus had to be a deity for me to love him. I have an attachment to Jesus like I have to William James and Thomas Jefferson. They're my heroes. My definition of God is a force far more powerful and complicated than a brain could understand.

Over the years I've become a Unitarian. I'm very proud of it. It's a very tolerant religion. I have basically said, "I won't join any religion that renounces others." I spent a long time getting out of a religion that renounces others, so the last thing I want to do is get back into a religion that does the same thing. I was worried that Judaism would say we are the Chosen People and the only right religion and everyone else is wrong. (Some religions want to wipe out other religions.)

That was probably my most joyful discovery when I began to learn about Judaism. I never would have dreamed that Judaism would be so close to my soul. (You assume that all religions are narrow-minded because yours was.) When dating a Jew, I know there's the assumption among many Christians that there would be no good reasons to convert to Judaism, and if you're doing it, it would be for the wrong reasons—just to make your partner happy.

Here's the way I look at it: Spiritually, I've always been a Unitarian. To me Judaism is a cherished part of Unitarianism. It's like saying, I'm an American, and now I'm going to choose a state to live in, e.g., the state of California. I do know that if Doug were Catholic, I wouldn't have converted to Catholicism. So even though I'm converting for him, it's only because I believe in it. I may not have found my way to Judaism without Doug, but I'm glad I did. In a way I've always sort of felt Jewish from birth because of all the Old Testament lessons I memorized—so instead of changing religions, I feel I'm just shedding bad parts of the religion I was born in. And I'm overwhelmed by the emotional embracing I've received when people find out that I'm becoming a Jew.

When I began to study Judaism, I didn't think I was going to change anything in my heart or my beliefs. In some ways I had a lot of discomfort—I didn't know if Judaism was going to be a lot of hocus-pocus. I had thought, I'll learn about your religion, but I don't think I ever thought it was truly going to be *my* religion. The main thing that changed in me was that I became humbled, inspired, by this people, the Jewish people. I feel as if there's never been such a successful, moral group, that there's never been another people who have stuck to and refused to abandon their principles and made that work. They're still here. I'm not sure I ever will feel *completely* Jewish though. I'll feel honored to be welcomed into the family of Judaism, but I'll feel like an adopted child. No matter how much I may wish I were Jewish, it's not my history; it's not my story.

Yet there may be some Judaism in my bloodline; my mom's maternal grandmother was part Swiss and part German. My grandmother corresponds with relatives in Switzerland. A lot was lost in translation, but she picks up that they practiced Judaism at some point. If that proves to be the case, I wouldn't feel like a wanna-be. I could share in the pride of being part of the lineage that survived for thousands of years. I could be a Jew two times over—by blood and by conviction. It would make me feel better, because you know how it is when you admire something but can't take any credit for it? Now I would feel like it was my own birthright, not just Doug's.

I think that from the get-go, the universe works in bizarre ways; that if I designed it, it wouldn't work that way, i.e., having to kill a plant or an animal for food. The world is so strange that it's clear that whatever our human desire might be, we aren't the be-all and end-all of the universe. At least I know I'm not going to understand it. (As a college student I was full of angst about all this.)

When I pray to God I have no idea if God is listening, and I don't mind if God's not (I could understand a world where there's a God who had better things to do). But if God is listening, my sense is God's very happy with my entrance into Judaism.

Doug Speaks

I like being Jewish. I went to Hebrew school, had a Bar Mitzvah, went to Israel every year; all this is a big deal in our family. All along I thought it would be better to marry someone who was Jewish, but I thought it was wrong to limit myself to certain groups. It didn't feel like the difference in religion should be the be-all and end-all. I had dated women who weren't Jewish before. My parents made clear what their values were, but they didn't say, and they would never say, you can't date someone; that was not the way they parented. I admire the way they raised us. Bottom line, they mentioned conversion once or twice when they knew we were serious.

It was hard meeting Jill's parents. I think they know I'm Jewish, although it was never explicit. I felt uneasy most of the time I was there. I sensed they had this Midwestern uneasiness with the East Coast. I feel like a lot was not talked about, not understood, as if we were from two different countries. I feel bad because it's their loss, a shortcoming, an inability. They make facile, mistaken characterizations of people. It really makes me angry, the way Jill's father treated her, his failure to be a father to her, not treating her and her mother like people really. However, you don't see that side of Jill's father when you meet him; it's not on display for you.

The fact that Jill is converting means a lot to me. I was very pleasantly surprised. I know she's doing it for me, though I tried not to put any pressure on her. If Jill didn't convert, we would have been married anyway. The big issue for me is how our kids are raised. We talked about it a lot, what the kids would be. Judaism has provided me with a value system that I know I want to pass on. Now I know our children will be brought up in a Jewish way.

Jill's Conversion

After my conversion I felt much more Jewish than I ever expected to feel. Instead of feeling like an adopted child, the way I assumed I would feel, I felt much more like a legitimate part of the Jewish people. It's like when someone hands you your diploma; you feel like you've earned something. At that moment you feel differently; you could never feel that way before.

One thing I didn't anticipate was that I had to walk past Doug, his parents and my friend Stephanie. I had just received the blessings of the rabbis, and I had such a feeling of happiness, yet I didn't dare look at them because I was afraid I would start crying. I didn't want to break down because I had to focus (I had to say the blessings the right way). Afterwards, with all the hugging and kissing, I couldn't stop the tears.

Later we went to the Four Seasons for dinner. The most overwhelming moment was when my future in-laws gave me a ring as a conversion gift, a precious family heirloom worn by Doug's grandmother her whole life. I was so overtaken that they would consider me so much a member of their family that I couldn't speak. I was totally silent. It was so heart-warming, the kindness of the rabbis, the kindness of Doug and his family. I had this feeling of self-consciousness; it was hard to believe it, almost as if I didn't deserve it. My instant instinct is that now that I'm Jewish, I've got much to learn. I've got to get better at Hebrew and at my prayers. I've got to become a better Jew.

FIVE

"Thank God I Married This Non-Jewish Woman"

Ellen and Joshua's Remarkable Metamorphosis

Of the several hundred students I have taught, none have embarked on such an incredible journey as Ellen, along with her husband, Joshua. He came from a Jewish family with little connection to Jewish observance. Ellen came from an Asian-American family who practiced Christianity. But as they entered the world of Judaism together through study and practice, the liberal approach to Judaism proved not to be enough. They hungered for something more, something that would dramatically transform every aspect of their lives.

When Ellen took those first tentative steps into my office a few years ago, I gazed upon a beautiful and bright young Japanese-American woman who was very apprehensive about encountering Judaism, the faith of her husband. Not at all interested in considering conversion, she was, however, willing to learn about her husband's faith for the sake of their future children. Her instincts told her they would be better off growing up with a single religious heritage, and they had agreed that it would be Judaism.

As we began to study, I easily saw Ellen's kindness. She was very warm, natural, unaffected, and unusually calm. In fact, when she left my office I, too, felt calm.

Most of the time Joshua studied along with her. At first Joshua did not understand why he couldn't have a Santa Claus come down the chimney of his home on Christmas Eve—after all, that was the way he grew up. But Ellen grasped right away the inconsistency and inappropriateness of such a custom for a Jewish family. Her thinking process seemed logical, while his position struck both of us as odd.

As the months progressed, Ellen decided Judaism was a religion and tradition that she could embrace, and she chose to undergo a conversion to Conservative Judaism. Yet this would be only the beginning for Ellen and Joshua. She had set the pace, but now his eyes were opened to the value of a religious life. Instead of eating sandwiches in front of the TV on Friday nights, they started to observe Shabbat, rejoicing in its beauty and relaxation.

Never in my wildest dreams would I have predicted that they would continue their journey into Judaism deep into the Orthodox tradition. Here, in Ellen's own words, is her remarkable story.

A Japanese Jew: "The Rabbis Said God Made This Thing Happen"

Just as Joshua always was drawn to Asian women, for some reason I was always drawn to Jewish men. I seem to have this affinity for the Jewish people. Joshua and I met at the university when we were freshmen. At first we were just good friends, but gradually we fell in love and got engaged our senior year. Judaism was the last thing on our minds, as we were not really thinking about the future and how we would raise our children. Joshua had grown up in a Jewish Reform household, where his parents had held Passover seders and attended services on Rosh Hashanah and Yom Kippur. Yet he knew very little about his religion.

Although my grandparents were married by a Shinto priest, my family never attended any kind of temple or church. After thirty years in this country, they were really more American than Japanese, and they were very open-minded. However, we did celebrate the secular aspects of Christmas and Easter, and I once had a month of Methodist Sunday school. There was a Jewish family in my neighborhood in suburban Syracuse, but I had no idea what that meant other than the fact that they didn't celebrate Christmas.

Even when Joshua and I were married by a judge a few years after college, we didn't really focus on religion. Joshua just wanted to have something Jewish about the wedding, so he wore a yarmulke (skull cap) and stepped on the glass at the end of the ceremony. At the time we didn't really understand what that meant.

Ideally, my parents would have wanted me to meet and marry another Japanese, but they knew that was unlikely to happen in Syracuse or at my university. Their only objection to my marriage to Joshua was that we were both so young, only twenty-four at the time. Joshua's family had no qualms about the marriage. Not that it would have changed our minds about marrying each other, but I'm just grateful that we didn't run into problems with our parents. Joshua's brother also married a non-Jew.

When we got married, Joshua's mother said, "Keep

in the back of your mind how you're going to raise your children. You may think it's not important now, but it will be in the future."

We moved to Washington, D.C., where I became a media associate at the Children's Defense Fund until I had Max, our first child. Joshua worked for a congresswoman as a legislative assistant for four or five years, somehow during that time managing to squeeze in graduate school. After acquiring a master's degree in national-security issues, he became a lobbyist for the American Israel Public Affairs Committee (AIPAC), handling defense issues. His trips to Israel at least once a year would prove to be catalysts toward religious observance.

But even before I was pregnant with Max, I was the one, not Joshua, who became interested in Judaism, basically because I thought the Jewish holidays were wonderful. I don't know what it was exactly that was the impetus for me to become Jewish. I didn't have any real basis on which to compare religions. It was just that believing in something appealed to me, I loved Joshua and his family and I felt it was right to raise our children with some kind of religion. Although Joshua's belief was at the bare minimum, he seemed very pleased. The rabbis said God made this thing happen.

A friend referred us to Rabbi Weiss. The moment we met, I thought she was terrific. There is no doubt she is the reason why we have come as far as we have on the religious path. She is so enthusiastic, a real cheerleader for Judaism. I caught that bug from her, and Joshua did, too. After I went through the conversion, it wasn't "Good-bye, have a nice Jewish life." She continues to be our mentor and friend.

Mostly I met with Rabbi Weiss by myself, but Joshua came whenever he could. He began to realize how much he didn't know about his own tradition. He started reading and paying attention to what I was learning and would go with me to various synagogues to hear different rabbis. I had thought this would be my effort, but soon we started taking this journey together.

Originally, I envisioned that our Jewish involvement would be similar to that of Joshua's family—seders, Bar Mitzvahs, holidays, and that would be it. But as we learned more, we started to change our habits. We stopped eating bacon and gradually gave up shellfish. Soon we were keeping kosher, not strictly, but a kind of Conservative version. Rabbi Weiss never advocated one way over the other. In the beginning, I would have been more comfortable with Reform Judaism, but Joshua had already moved into the Conservative camp and was now headed down a faster track.

We spent a year in weekly study, immersing ourselves in many Jewish books, for example, *To Be a Jew, Your People/My People, On Jewish Holidays*, etc. I took a seven-week course in Hebrew. Throughout this process, I had never expected to connect with the spiritual side of Judaism. I never even imagined that there could be that spiritual connection. I guess I just didn't know what I was missing. The spiritual affects the family, the home, the synagogue, the community, how we interact with people in our everyday life. I never knew it could just seep into everything you do.

We joined a Conservative synagogue where we were very happy and where I felt welcome. We were keeping kosher, and although we drove on the Sabbath, we didn't cook or watch TV. But Joshua was moving forward religiously. He became worried that Max would not be considered Jewish by everyone, that the Orthodox would not accept his conversion (or mine). We spoke to a no-nonsense-type Orthodox rabbi who made it clear that there was no shortcut, no simple way, of having an Orthodox conversion just for Max. It would necessitate our commitment to an Orthodox lifestyle. Meanwhile, on one of his business trips to Israel, Joshua spent Shabbat with an Orthodox family, came home raving about it, and said, "I want to become Orthodox."

I was like, "Wait a minute! We can't just jump into this headfirst." I envisioned the stereotypical people with black hats and a million kids. While I'm much more cautious than Joshua, I agreed to keep an open mind and was willing to see what it was like. I wondered if I would be comfortable, if the Orthodox would welcome me, someone who was clearly not Jewish by birth. Would they accept me? Or were they crazy people altogether? Part of me was apprehensive, and part of me was curious.

Our first experience was with a newly religious Orthodox family in a nearby city who could have been hippies in the 1960s. They were very laid-back and mellow, a lot of fun, and very open about their journey into Orthodoxy. There was nothing weird about them, except for the male's sidelocks and the black hats worn to shul (synagogue). Their kids were playing computer games like other kids. I thought, *Well, this isn't so bad. . . .*

We made the rounds of the different Orthodox communities in the area, and I found that modern Orthodoxy really appealed to me. It didn't seem that different from being Conservative. It seemed very welcoming, very comfortable. My Japanese background was not at all an issue. Since you really can't experience Orthodox Judaism without living in an

Orthodox community, we decided to move to an Orthodox neighborhood. A townhouse opened up in a suburban community and we moved in eight months ago. Everyone was so terrific; it felt right immediately. We moved when I was seven months pregnant with our second child, Miriam. Someone said, "Think about an Orthodox conversion before the baby is born."

The idea of community is so wonderful. Everyone is so supportive; they go out of their way for you; neighbors look out for each other. It is so special and heartwarming to know your neighbors will be there for you in good times and bad. I had something similar to that growing up, but here we had something in common with the neighbors as well—the common bond of keeping kosher, of celebrating holidays centered around the home; it ties you together. We have had a lot of fun since we've moved here.

Since we were already living an Orthodox lifestyle, an Orthodox conversion would be a formality. In the space of one week, I got an Orthodox conversion, got married by an Orthodox rabbi and had a baby. The day before the Orthodox wedding, Joshua was to receive an ufruf in the synagogue (a special honor for the groom on the eve of his wedding), but on his way to shul (synagogue) he was called away. The rabbi announced from the pulpit that a groom had been scheduled for an ufruf, but unfortunately the bride went into labor!

We scheduled the Orthodox conversion and wedding on October 26, my parents' anniversary, which they appreciated. It was the icing on the cake for us to be married by an Orthodox rabbi. I had come full circle. That day all of us went to the mikvah (ritual bath). I pledged to undertake kashrut (dietary laws), keep the Sabbath and uphold the laws of family purity. I immersed and then ran off to the synagogue to be married before sixty or seventy people, including our kids. I had felt Jewish all along, personally and emotionally, but the conversion ceremonies were private. The wedding was the final public acceptance. It was wonderful.

My parents thought it was a little weird at first. Joshua and I love food and had always enjoyed going out to restaurants and indulging ourselves. Now we were limited. Our parents couldn't believe we could actually stick to keeping kosher. They thought we would miss shellfish, but they did think keeping the Sabbath was commendable.

My parents own a Japanese restaurant, and when my children visit they can't eat there. But there are ways to control the food preparation, and there are kosher

Japanese products. Now we don't view it as a hardship, or as an issue, so they're cool with it. They accept it. They know we don't travel on Friday and Saturday.

Joshua's father had thought that becoming a Conservative Jew was crazy. Our Orthodoxy baffled him even more. Joshua puts on tefillin (phylacteries) and goes to the synagogue three times on the Sabbath. "You go to synagogue every Saturday? Why?" my father-in-law would ask. "It's not necessary. You don't have to take the laws so literally." He has since somewhat come to terms with our decision, but he is against our placing the children in a Jewish day school. He feels we are putting blinders on, isolating ourselves, and to a certain extent he may be right. Joshua's wearing of the kippah (skullcap) and tzitzis (fringes of the prayer shawl) in public bothers his father; he feels it's screaming to the world that you're Jewish. But my mother-in-law is fine with it; she had an Orthodox upbringing as a child, but rejected it. I'm sure she thinks we're a little bit nuts, but she doesn't voice objections.

This is the fourth year of our journey into Judaism. I never would have imagined that I would be Orthodox. I guess you never know where life will lead you. My mind is open, but it is more likely that I could move in an even more Orthodox direction than go the other way. At the time of my conversion into Conservative Judaism, I thought it was the ultimate religious experience. Now I know I was only partly there. What I have now, in the Orthodox tradition, is the epitome, the zenith, compared to what I had then. You have to not just accept but also act upon your faith and your beliefs, if you believe there is a greater purpose. I have found something that gives a deeper meaning to my life than just going through the day, a spiritual element to everything I do. I am constantly reminded of what God has given us, which we shouldn't take for granted: the food we eat, the children we have. There is a reason for it, there is definitely a Higher Being here, even if we don't always agree with everything God does. If we live by the commandments we will be rewarded in the world to come; we all have to do our part.

I see so much joy in Judaism. It's such a rich tradition. And while I feel American, I still don't want to let myself forget my ethnic Japanese background; Max's middle name is Chiune, the name of the Japanese envoy who saved so many Jews during the Holocaust. It's a good way to join the two traditions. But on the level of soul, I do feel that I have a Jewish soul. I feel I am a Japanese Jew. That's what I am.

"Thank God I Married This Non-Jewish Woman"

Immediately following the Orthodox conversion of Ellen and their two children, Ellen and Joshua had an Orthodox wedding to sanctify their marriage within the Orthodox tradition. After Ellen emerged from the mikvah (ritual bath), Joshua said she looked more beautiful than ever. She wore white, with a white veil, for the wedding ceremony. Joshua held their son, Max, while Ellen circled Joshua the traditional seven times. "Thank God I married this non-Jewish woman; it was she who brought me back to Judaism," Joshua proclaimed. "Her soul was at Sinai. She found her way back through the clouds."

"This is a miracle," said the Orthodox rabbi who performed the ceremony. "It's a crazy mixture of coincidence." He went on to say that as descendants of Noah, we all get another chance, another opportunity, a new beginning. "You are an inspiration to all of us. It was meant to be," he said. "God made this day. God made this happen." Joshua and Ellen fought back tears. It was only a short time before that Joshua had found God. But now he recognized that God had been with him "the whole time." On his face he wore the innocent expression of a Bar Mitzvah boy.

*At one time, Joshua knew very little about Israel,
the land of his ancestors, but today he is a lobbyist for
the American Israel Public Affairs Committee. What
is so fascinating to me about Joshua is that he uses
Torah portions, uses a vocabulary previously totally
unfamiliar to him, to guide his life and his family.
Home from a business trip to Israel and filled with
enthusiasm to assume the Orthodox lifestyle, he worried that Ellen would call the lawyers, call the psy-
chiatrists. Instead, Ellen moved with him into an
Orthodox neighborhood and found it right for both of
them. "So many people have helped us reach this
point," Joshua told me. "It's not that the miracles just
started; it's that we've just noticed."*

SIX

She Came to Learn, Not to Convert

Laura's Insatiable Quest

 *One afternoon I went out for bagels with Adam, the son of an old friend, a very bright young man with a Ph.D. in applied mathematics. Being a Jew was important to Adam, and he confessed how conflicted he was about marrying a non-Jewish woman named Laura. I gave Adam my e-mail address just in case Laura, who at the time was teaching at the University of Chicago, would care to contact me.*

So Laura and I first introduced ourselves over e-mail. When she came to Washington to meet Adam's family, we chatted in my office. Laura struck me as a very warm and kind young woman who was unusually intelligent—a good match for Adam. She made it quite clear that she was not interested in converting to Judaism. When I assured her that it is not my aim to convert anyone, but simply to expose them to the

Jewish religious tradition, she seemed much relieved.

At the same time I could see that her natural curiosity was aroused. She was very verbal and asked me many questions about Adam's religious background. That was the key to Laura. She wanted to better understand the man she was going to marry by learning about his faith and culture. In fact, she is one of the few people I have encountered who intuitively understood just how important that is in a marriage. Armed with books on Judaism, Laura went back to Chicago just willing to think about the possibility of studying with me when she eventually would move to Washington.

Just how far Laura has come from those early contacts astounds both of us today. Now thirty-one, Laura is one whom I am encouraging to further her Jewish education with the possibility of attending rabbinical school. A natural teacher already (she teaches English at a prestigious private school), she is both tolerant and compassionate and has the depth, intellect and ability to make a wonderful rabbi.

I feel such pride in Laura as she embraces a tradition she understands from the heart as well as from the intellect. She has a knowledge of our roots and heritage, but it's more than that. The Jewish spirit is deeply imbedded in her. She can quote from the Bible, talk about Talmud and Midrash, and she lives it, attending synagogue regularly and keeping a kosher home.

What happened to Laura to transform her from a curious observer into a deeply committed Jew?

Laura "Would Not Convert"

Adam and I were married a year ago by a judge with some Jewish practices incorporated into the ceremony. We had met in graduate school at the University of Chicago, where I was an English major and he was studying mathematics. Adam is Jewish, but at the time he never suggested I convert to Judaism. And I, in fact, was saying that I would not convert. It seemed to me then that it would be like giving up my identity. At any rate, he never asked—and I'm glad he didn't. Even so, it would have been fine with me to have a rabbi conduct the wedding, but it would have been very hard on my parents if no minister were present. Something so different from their tradition would have been difficult for them to witness.

As for me, for some reason I never actually prayed to Jesus when growing up, even though I was raised in a religious Protestant family, attended church every Sunday and played piano for the choir every Wednesday. I had always addressed God directly. The whole idea of hell and original sin and the need for Jesus to redeem us was troubling to me. So by the time I attended college, even though I continued to believe in God, I simply stopped believing in Jesus and attended church only when I had the chance to sing solos (I was studying voice at the time).

When I met Adam, he was not really a practicing Jew, although he had a Bar Mitzvah. Yet he wanted his children to be Jewish for the sake of continuity of the culture. I vowed I would never put my children through the difficulties faced when there's a mixed marriage, so I agreed to raise our children Jewish. Besides, I no longer considered myself a Christian. With its emphasis on learning, assertiveness and ethics, Judaism would have been my choice for my children anyway. The Talmudic tradition of arguing and discussing and learning by questioning instead of by merely listening was very appealing to me. Now I was in need of some knowledge about the Jewish tradition, which eventually led me to Rabbi Weiss's study.

Rabbi Weiss is an old friend of Adam's family, and she and I hit it off immediately. At the beginning of instruction she states that she doesn't convert people, only shares her love for the tradition. That was very important to me at the time. I was a little skittish. Had she been unfriendly or discouraging, I would have stayed away. Being welcomed help me get over that hurdle.

Learning about Judaism was something Adam and I decided to do together. That made me feel like there was nothing wrong with me in particular that needed to be fixed. We acquired a broad understanding by exploring a list of thirty books spanning the tradition from the very liberal to the Orthodox. I had always felt the intellect was played down in Christianity; it was enough just to believe, not necessarily understand. By contrast, Judaism seemed so intellectual: It felt good to have an intellect and use it.

When Rabbi Weiss taught the ethics unit, I perceived that what felt alien at first was, in fact, what I always had wanted to believe. Christianity's emphasis was not on this world, but on transcending it. Not so with Judaism. In Judaism, everything is elaborately spelled out, describing in detail the way that is ethical.

I began attending services at a Conservative congregation on Saturday mornings. Adam went with me at first, but he never got into it. A class in Hebrew helped me, but it still took about three months to feel comfortable with the prayerbook. It has become a real spiritual experience for me. Amazingly, now that I understand the prayers, I realize I am praying to the same God I had always prayed to in the past.

I started to adopt some traditional Jewish practices, like keeping kosher. We were already vegetarian, so the transition was quite easy. I'm also studying, practicing and trying to observe Shabbat—no shopping and no schoolwork (I teach English) on Saturday. Every observant, religious Jew whom I have encountered has been both encouraging and happy for me as I have adopted these traditions. That has made a big difference. Other Jews who are nonobservant think I'm crazy for practicing the customs and laws. "Why would you want to do that?" they ask. They haven't chosen to practice Judaism for themselves, so they wonder why anyone else would.

I did it because the more I practiced, the more it really felt good and natural and right. One day at services, I was feeling sad at being an outsider and wanted to be like everyone else. Then it dawned on me that it was possible; it had been building in me. Practicing Jewish traditions, living that way, made the difference. I told Rabbi Weiss I wanted to become a Jew. She wanted me to be sure of my decision and to make certain the decision was all mine, not anyone else's. Adam, of course, was not surprised. He had already guessed before I even announced it. My in-laws were incredibly happy, but I didn't tell my parents until Christmas when I could speak to them face to face. That was painful, but they took it as well as possible. I do feel sad that this change for me is hard for my mother. At the time of my conversion, she was grieving for my grandfather, and I thought, *She doesn't need more* tsuris *(grief)*. Yet she sent me flowers and is genuinely happy for me.

I underwent a Conservative (rather than a Reform) conversion because I wanted my conversion to be accepted by more people. It was different from what I expected. A Bet Din (rabbinical court) composed of three Conservative rabbis questioned me in the library of a school. In that venue, it felt more like part of daily life, part of the community. It was very moving to say the blessings in the mikvah (ritual bath). It reminded me of the speech-action theory, that just by saying a word, you cause an action to happen, for example, "The Lord said, 'Let there be light.'" Saying those blessings in the mikvah was like that; I was making myself Jewish. For continuity's sake, I chose the Hebrew name Miriam, since the biblical Miriam was a singer—like me. After I affirmed my faith, and that I had chosen to join the Jewish people, I asked God's help. Then I said the Shema, the watchword of the people of Israel. It was amazing ending with that. The tears came. On the way home, I bought a mezuzah for my door. In June we will visit Israel.

The first time I lit the Shabbat candles as a Jew, it really did feel like a miracle. It is the same blessing Jewish women have said for thousands of years, and the miracle of light is the same. But I was scared that something would go wrong and the candles would go out. Yet, when I uncovered my eyes, there were the flames, burning brightly. I am happy and feel privileged to choose to join the family of Judaism, and I thank you, God, for having chosen me.

Laura's mother-in-law was present at Laura's conversion ceremony. She says, "It was extremely moving to be outside the room when Laura recited the prayers. She did not know I was standing right there. It was a level of commitment for Laura to my son and his family that is really momentous, deep and powerful. It was not for show, but clearly very serious on her part. I had been concerned that the Jewish religious tradition continue to the next generation, and this was the assurance for me that it would happen."

SEVEN

We Want to Be
a Jewish Family

Peter and Danielle's Gift

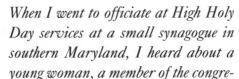 *When I went to officiate at High Holy
Day services at a small synagogue in
southern Maryland, I heard about a
young woman, a member of the congre-
gation, who was very sick in the hospital. I wondered
who she was and why she was so sick. I decided to pay
her a visit, even if nobody requested it.*

*When I first saw Danielle, she had just been
released from intensive care and had tubes in her
arms. After years of trying to have a baby, she had
almost died during an operation resulting from com-
plications of pregnancy. Her husband was sitting in a
chair by her bed. Coming from a rural area where so
few Jews lived, she was overwhelmed that a rabbi had
come to see her in a time of need. Yet I had not really
given it much thought; I just came. We talked about
life and how much she appreciated being alive. It was*

83

a very emotional and very powerful beginning of a deep friendship. She asked for books on Jewish life-cycle events and for prayers that could be said for the death of an unborn fetus. I gave her some writings that proved helpful. At the same time, I got to know her husband, Peter.

Peter had converted to Judaism before they got married, but he felt like an outsider because he thought he didn't know enough about his new faith. He yearned to feel like he really belonged. He and Danielle enrolled in classes I held at their synagogue and then continued to study with me privately. Eventually he asked me to prepare him for a more traditional conversion.

The couple lived in a county where the Ku Klux Klan had been dominant in the not-too-distant past. Most people on the street or in the shopping center had never met a Jew and knew nothing of Jewish practices. To be a Jew in such an environment is not easy. It is not surprising that the area's tiny synagogue had been closed for many years.

Yet now there were people who were trying to rejuvenate it, paying the utilities just so it could stay open. Peter and Danielle joined them. Suddenly, building the Jewish community became a very important part of their lives.

Some time later, they had a miracle baby, their own

biological child, born from a host mother. It was overwhelming to see Peter participate equally with Danielle in their son's Brit Milah (covenant of circumcision). Peter took it upon himself to acquire more knowledge; it produced a comfort level for him. He said prayers by himself as well as with Danielle, sipped the wine and, alone, spoke of the meaning and importance of having their son. He was beside himself with joy and so proud to be part of the Jewish community.

A large crowd of personal friends—members of both the Jewish and non-Jewish community—were awed and moved by Peter's warm welcoming of this new gift of life: a Jewish child. Now Peter walks into the synagogue with a tallit (prayer shawl) and yarmulke (head covering) and feels very much at home. He adores his Jewish wife and child, and to be closer to them he wanted to be bonded into a family unit. This was the way.

Peter's Affinity for Jewish People

During my sophomore year in college, I was sitting in a pizza shop. At a nearby table, some Jewish girls were talking. Two guys commented that they should be put in ovens. I threatened the men and chased them out the door. I guess I have had an affinity for Jewish people. It just happened that 90 percent of the women I've dated were Jewish. It was purely physical attraction, animal instincts.

I grew up in a rural area of Maryland, where I spent my youth racing motorcycles and dirt bikes. In high school I took a class on comparative religion that exposed me to Judaism, but the whole time I was growing up, I only knew three Jewish families (through sports teams I was on). There weren't more than ten Jewish families in the whole county. When I got to the University of Maryland, it was quite a surprise because there were lots of Jewish students.

By the time I met Danielle, I hadn't been in church in twenty years. My dad died when I was nine, but religion was never high on the agenda when he was alive, and my mother never went to church. She has no problems with my becoming Jewish; in fact, she embraces it. It so happens that today a number of her business partners and good friends are Jewish.

At first Danielle's father was upset that I wasn't Jewish. After she brought me home for dinner, he told her, "I never want him back again." But later he warmed up and paid for a terrific wedding. I felt close to him.

Danielle mentioned she wanted her children raised in the Jewish faith; that was fine with me. On one side, I had the most beautiful and caring woman I had ever met, who requested that her future generations inherit a rich heritage. On the other side was a religion to which I felt no ties. But it struck me that it would be hard to raise Jewish children if you have no idea what it's about. So it was my idea to take conversion classes in a classroom setting. We live in southern Maryland, so I had to drive ninety miles each way once a week. I wanted to undergo a Conservative Jewish conversion because it would be accepted by more Jews, but the rabbi said two words to me that brought terror to my heart: Brit Milah, the ritual circumcision that every Jewish male undergoes. So I opted to go the Reform route since a Reform conversion didn't require this procedure. All this I did before Danielle and I got married because we wanted to be married in a Reform synagogue. I did this for both of us, for Danielle and me, because we wanted a Jewish wedding and Jewish children.

I've felt Jewish for a long time now and I'm proud of being a Jew. There's a lot of warmth in the Jewish family and in the traditions; there are a lot of family-oriented activities, lots of holidays. Practically everything is centered around the family. It's a shame that a lot of the world doesn't see or understand it.

Some time before our son was born, we looked into hiring a mohel (one who is trained to perform the ritual circumcision). But the mohel we contacted (we were told he was the best) was not satisfied with my Reform conversion; he wouldn't let me fully participate in the ceremony as the father. I could have looked for another mohel, but I was so awed by my son's anticipated birth (he's truly a miracle baby), that I was inspired to take private instruction in Judaism from Rabbi Weiss and undergo a Conservative conversion. So I had a ritual circumcision after all. I finally decided to grin and bear it. The same mohel who would circumcise my son performed it.

Both Danielle and I began to study privately with Rabbi Weiss because we wanted to know more. When I finally went before the Bet Din (a rabbinical court comprised of three rabbis) for my Conservative conversion, the rabbis smiled when I told them I was there for an upgrade. But it was very serious and very emotional for me. You immerse yourself completely nude in the mikvah (ritual bath) in warm water. When you're all wet, you say prayers. My father-in-law came and stood with the rabbis in a nearby room. That meant a lot to me. And afterwards, of course, we went to the deli for some good Jewish food.

I didn't have much religion before; I was more an agnostic. So I didn't feel as if I were giving something up to become Jewish; I felt as if I were finding something. I really embraced it. I believe in what religion offers humanity. Without it, we would be a chaotic species.

Judaism has enhanced my life tremendously—although the holidays have interrupted a couple of really nice vacations! Judaism has given Danielle and me something we both focus on. Most Friday nights and on all the holidays, we attend synagogue. I never thought I could be so close to a religion as I am to Judaism. It brings me close to my wife, close to my son. His birth has opened up emotions in me I never knew I had.

Danielle Speaks

I always grew up thinking I was going to marry someone Jewish; I was never given a choice or an option. In high school I can remember falling head over heels with a non-Jew and my mother losing sleep over it and having bad dreams. "If a Jewish boy asks you out, you have to take that date," she argued. We were not observant, but culturally, ethnically, we identified as Jews.

In college I dated mostly Jewish boys, but after college I was at loose ends, so I decided to try living and working with my dad in southern Maryland, an area with a sparse Jewish population. My great-grandfather had been a peddler from Baltimore who moved there. So my father grew up Jewish in a very Catholic society. He was proud of being a Jew but experienced prejudice and was called a "Christ killer" as early as the first grade. His link to Judaism was as a persecuted underdog, and his vindication came later when he became known as the most visible Jew and one of the most successful businesspeople in the region.

Here I was, a Jewish woman at the end of the earth in southern Maryland. I found someone to date who was Jewish, but he wasn't a nice person. At that point I said to myself, "You can't settle for someone just because he's Jewish, just because you're isolated." I didn't want to settle; I just needed time to figure out what I was looking for. I was at this evaluation period in my life when Peter and I met. The first time I invited Peter to dinner, my dad threw a fit. "That's the first and last time you're bringing somebody who's not Jewish to sit at my dinner table," he said. But Peter was so charming, so warm and interested in what my dad said, and so funny, that his initial reservations soon dissipated.

We spent a lot of time dating at arm's length, first forming a really nice friendship, because instinctively on my part there were limits and boundaries in our relationship since he wasn't Jewish. But he was so handsome, funny, charming and adventuresome. When our relationship got more serious, I let him know from the beginning how strongly I felt about being Jewish. If we had a family, I wanted a Jewish family, and he would have to learn about Judaism. We agreed on it.

It was enlightening to me to study Judaism as well. While I had gone to Sunday school and Hebrew school, I had been a rebellious student and didn't learn much. Now I couldn't help Peter understand if I knew nothing myself.

Peter's conversion to Judaism was a big gift to me and my family. My mother was beside herself, and there was a big celebration after the ceremony. Dad even gave Peter the Jewish star ring he wore.

Living active Jewish lives has provided an important affiliation for us in our little community. It is almost surreal; I never imagined it would be this way. The synagogue has grown to forty families; there's a Judaism class, a thrift store, Torah study, a hundred people at a community Passover seder. It's pretty astounding.

The synagogue has become my extended family. I never realized to what extent this was true until my father passed away last year. We didn't have room for all the food and cakes members of the congregation brought to our house. The amount of support we received was incredible. We were completely blown away by it.

I may not have been as involved in our synagogue or come as far on this religious journey had Peter been born a Jew. Because to help him learn, I had to learn myself. We really are practicing Jews; we are both on this quest to create a Jewish family.

The more Peter and I deepen our knowledge of Judaism, the more equipped we are to be the parents of a Jewish child. I definitely believe in God, especially since the birth of our son. Morning, noon and night we thank God for him.

EIGHT

Conquering a Bitter Past

Anna's Triumph

Anna was very nervous, almost afraid to talk when she walked into my office five years ago. But she was interested in her husband's father's Jewish background, and she wanted to learn more about it, to explore it. I wasn't surprised, really. Often when there is some Jewish thread that is found in one partner's history, an intelligent, curious person looks into it. An artist and writer, Anna was looking for something to obtain meaning in life, something she missed in her own very troubled upbringing.

What struck me about Anna was her insecurity about herself; she was almost afraid of her own shadow. She had no sense of confidence whatsoever. Yet I saw this lovely and unaffected woman as extremely bright, brilliant even, with tremendous insight and compassion. There was something

remarkable about her, something that couldn't get free.
Dark shadows from her past were imprisoning her.

That is what is so amazing about the learning
process that we went through together. Anna just blos-
somed like a flower. I gave her encouragement in her
study of Judaism, and she drew strength from acquiring knowledge. She delved into books—but not like
just anybody would do. The more I gave her, the more
she wanted to go into greater depth, to examine the
technical source materials and decipher the actual text
in detail. Through her studies she gained the confidence
to try things on her own, like making a Shabbat dinner. Her husband, a photographer and curator at a
major museum, worked long hours, and it was a
struggle to pull it off. But when she did, she felt good,
because it brought them closer together and gave her a
purpose and framework for living. I encouraged her
to go to services, too. That first year, she passed out
books on the High Holy Days and felt like she was
part of the community, like she had a place to go, even
if she went by herself. I'll never forget when Anna
decided to try making a Passover seder. By this time
her husband was no longer bucking her or fighting her.
How she enjoyed it!

For a long time Anna had feared she would not
make a fit mother, which was mind-boggling to me. I

kept telling her just the opposite, that she would make a terrific mother. But she was already in her late thirties, and she and her husband planned not to have any children due to her anxiety. Soon Anna was going regularly to services. As we studied the units on prayer and the meaning of life, it helped her realize her own validity, her own goodness. Gradually she learned not to doubt herself so much. By the time she was ready to go to the mikvah (ritual bath) for conversion, she confided to me that she had gained enough self-confidence to have a child. She went to the mikvah and two weeks later called to say, "Rabbi, I'm pregnant!"

Anna's son, David, is a beautiful child, and her husband gladly spends time at home helping with the baby. Anna's husband is also a wonderful person—kind, caring and very intelligent. Anna has given him a rekindling of his heritage on his father's side; she has brought it alive to him, and they celebrate it together. It is a pleasure to be around them both. Of course, they held a bris (ritual circumcision) for David, and the family regularly celebrates Shabbat and other Jewish holidays. Anna had a Bat Mitzvah of her own and has become a real Jewish scholar.

Today I see a woman who laughs, who is not afraid to give you a kiss and who is so well respected in her synagogue community that she leads part of the services. I am in awe of this transformed person. Now that she has found herself through her faith, what a gift she brings to the Jewish community!

Anna: I Tried to Have No Past

It is very hard to be part of any community when shame and guilt shatter your own family. There is a gap between you and the rest of the world. I used to look at other people and look at their lives and wonder about them, just like you wonder about the story behind the Easter Island heads. It was a complete mystery to me how others lived.

I tried to have no past, to cut myself off from my own history, but that didn't work at all. When my mother was killed (I was twenty-eight), I became very depressed. I withdrew, thinking it was my fault that she was dead. I couldn't let go of the idea that I was unable—that I failed—to help her (she was an alcoholic). You need forgiveness to move forward.

I had been working very hard writing documentaries about artists with my husband. Then suddenly that was over and I wasn't busy and distracted anymore.

I started facing my own feelings. I had always been numb before; that was the way I got through the pain, but now I felt desperate. At thirty, it was time for me to face the past and deal with my emotions. But it took awhile to open up.

It helped to join an organization for family and friends of alcoholics. I started to feel that there was some kind of God. I began to believe. I wanted to be strong and let go of my mother. That was the first time I prayed. Although my mother had been dead for some time, I was stuck, still trying to get her sober; I couldn't let go. I prayed that if God was there, I wanted Him to help me let go and live my life and do who knows what.

I realized then that I couldn't cope anymore on my own. It was moving and scary, and yet I also got a feeling of relief. I changed. I became calmer, more comfortable and more at ease. I learned how to meditate, how to pray—not with a Christian orientation though, just prayer. Now I was better able to relate to other people and to unload my resentment, anger and rage. I realized I was not alone, that there were others who were ashamed also.

At the time, I was very interested in different religions and cultures, although personally I had been adverse to religion. I had not believed in God when I was growing up, and I certainly hadn't been looking for God. I never really found anything that didn't strike me as flaky, for example, New Age religion or Zen Buddhism. In the late 1970s the University of Santa Clara, where I was attending school, was a mecca for that kind of thing. I met a lot of Jews there searching for God everywhere but in their own religion.

By a strange and moving coincidence, I was reviewing my life at the time of Yom Kippur and found myself picking up a Jewish prayerbook in a church whose cross had been covered over for a Jewish service. The prayerbook addressed precisely the same activity I was doing—taking stock, reviewing the past. I felt a shock of recognition, a discovery in this church. I wanted to join with other like-minded people, Jewish people.

At this point I took a survey course on Judaism, spoke to different rabbis and was referred to Rabbi Weiss. I felt comfortable with her right away. I wasn't young or getting married; I was already married. There was no ostensible reason for converting; I was just so happy to pursue Judaism. That's how I felt from the beginning.

I had always read a lot of history and knew quite a bit about the Holocaust and that era. It's amazing to me that such things were simply not talked about in school. There was a Christmas pageant, but no Jewish observations. The Jews knew about Christians, but the Christians knew very little about the Jews. Yet as a child I was very curious about the Jews mentioned in the Jesus stories. I remember seeing a Hanukkah menorah in a friend's house, and her mother explained it to me very seriously when I was about eight.

During a year of study I practiced becoming a Jew. There's a point in the journey when you're not really anything. It's frightening. You are on the journey, but you haven't arrived yet. I felt I was on this journey, but who was I going to be? It was awesome. What was I going to be like? It's daunting, embarrassing even, the older you are, to start over, to learn the Aleph-Bet, and to do something brand-new in middle age. Right after I converted, I realized now I have to do certain things: Now I'm obligated.

But I wrestle and struggle; I have setbacks. I feel the need to reach out to my brother, from whom I have been estranged, even if he doesn't want me. Sometimes it feels frustrating. On Yom Kippur, I know I'll look back on what I've made of my year. The main thing I feel is that I'm part of something that will outlive me; I feel God is what is eternal.

My Hebrew name, Eliana, means "my God has

answered me." Rabbi Weiss helped me pick that name. Sometimes the answer comes before the question, but I feel God knows what is best for me. I wasn't seeking to become a Jew really, and this avenue just opened up. You don't expect it—I'm stuck in my place and it opens up to me like the Red Sea did before Moses. It's meaningful to me that I can give an eternal gift like Judaism to somebody else, to my own child. It's amazing to me, in fact; I never would have dreamed something like that.

There are things that nobody knows about me. I never thought I would have children. I was actually terrified to become a mother because I knew it would revive memories of my childhood and every-thing would flood back to me. I was very worried that I would fail. The hardest thing for me was to over-come that fear. I had been abandoned by my family from early childhood to be my alcoholic mother's caretaker, and I was constantly failing in that respon-sibility. Now it was frightening to me to be respon-sible for someone else. I had all this anxiety, and I was fearful that I would feel very trapped again. But I came to realize that it was possible that I could be a good mother. Rabbi Weiss talked to me about it. Of course I feel totally different now, since I had the baby. It was very healing to go through the process. I was so shocked, so incredibly joyful; this is totally unlike how I thought my life would be.

My husband, a photographer as well as a specialist in photography shows, wasn't religious at all, although from what he told me, I assumed he had some Jewish background. We never talked about it, really, for many years. We talked about the arts and artists rather than religion. Yet so many people in the art world and in the field of art history have been Jewish. It may have to do with literacy and with Jews focusing on education. Those values carry over from one field to the next. And the economics of it. The arts are professions you carry with you. Although I do very little right now as an artist myself, the closest thing I relate to is a Midrash, a Jewish story narrative. It can be fascinating to interpret a story with a collage. I'm interested in the characters in a story or in making images of ideas and symbols.

My journey to Judaism has been very dramatic for my husband because his family was so hostile to the religion even though his father is of Jewish descent. Apparently my in-laws got some flack when they got married; my father-in-law got flack from both communities. As a result, my general impression is that they don't like Jewish people. It can be a real strain when my father-in-law harangues or chides me about being a Jew. He has been quite angry about it. But since David was born, my in-laws have turned to mush. They send Santa Clauses. I tell them to send Chanukah presents, that we keep a Jewish home, but it has been hard because they exchange Christmas presents. They just have to understand that there is to be no confusion in our home. I'm very firm on that. Keeping both religions may work for parents but not for their kids, because the two cultures are really incompatible. The meaning is completely different, and it creates a split. I'm very clear at my house with David; he goes to a Jewish school, and he's very comfortable with who he is.

Today my husband is very supportive of my Judaism; he has learned a lot from what I have learned and how I practice. We always do Shabbat and have Friday night at home. My husband goes with me to services and to friends' houses for holidays. He is also taking some classes and has thought about converting himself. He well may do it. It is just that his father is so adamant, so negative, about it, and he feels it would be hurtful to his mother as well. She sent him to a Christian Sunday school.

There are some Jews who may like me but who don't think of me as a Jew because I was not born Jewish. In the kosher store (we keep kosher), I may wonder how many are looking at me as if I am not a Jew. The people I have had the most trouble with, however, are secular Jews, or women who resent me because they assume I have married a Jewish guy, and they have some anxiety about finding one themselves. My main thought is, if my son grows up and is not given any education in his Jewish heritage, that would be unacceptable, horrible really. I think he would suffer. It would make it very hard for him to approach Judaism and he might identify negatively, which happens if someone has no positive identity and is discriminated against. My son may not do what I do, but I think he will stay with it. I want to be a Jewish grandmother. That is my ambition.

I had encouraged Anna to remember her mother, however painful it would be, during the Yizkor service (a service remembering loved ones who are no longer with us) on Yom Kippur. "This Yom Kippur, your words came back to me," she wrote me in a note, "and I prayed from the prayer for remembering a mother, and cried, and felt that something was resolved for me. It felt like God expectantly said, 'Now remember your lesson with Rabbi Weiss. . . .'"

NINE

When You Can't Let Go of "Christ"

Meredith's Dilemma

Nobody has ever challenged me with such sensitive and provocative questions about Judaism as Meredith. She is so smart, so inquisitive; I'm amazed by her depth and her thought processes. Initially Meredith attended a class I taught on basic Judaism at the Jewish Community Center because she was curious about the religious background of her Jewish fiancé, Allen. Although he identified strongly as a Jew, Allen had never encouraged her. He was not observant of any of the traditions, and in the past had fought religious or Jewish community participation. Raised by his father in a farm town with few Jews, he was very young when his mother left the family home and converted from Judaism to Catholicism. He has a little girl from a first marriage to a gentile woman, and at this point, largely due to Meredith's influence,

he wants to pass on his Jewish heritage to her. It's like a bond between them.

Meredith herself was raised in a strict Catholic home and went to church often. Her family, especially her mother, is very strong in her religion. So here Meredith is now, with this Jewish man, who—while not traditional—is very Jewish in his thinking, in his being. "You're loving the man, you're touched by his religion," she once told me. Meredith felt that for the sake of the relationship, it was necessary for her to delve into his background. She knew intuitively the importance of this buried way of life to Allen, even if he never expressed it openly. She is very wise.

At our last group class, Allen came along. We talked, we felt a connection, and I accepted where he was in terms of his Jewishness. Next he volunteered to come to the class's Shabbat dinner, where he participated in some of the prayers. Meredith then decided to study further with me privately because she wanted to learn much more about Judaism. It has been a very powerful exploration for her—and for me—months of challenging, spiritually shaking questions fraught with tension over what it means to be a Jew. While she accepts the tenets of Judaism on an intellectual level and wants to raise Jewish children in a Jewish family, she herself cannot embrace Judaism because she fears losing her own identity. She can never go back to the way she was before, she says, and yet she cannot go forward. She cannot leave behind the "Christ" story of revelation in the New Testament. She cannot leave behind the "person of Jesus." Christ didn't fail her, she says; it was only the structure, the trappings, of her church that failed her. Moreover, Meredith feels guilty because her mother is upset that she is moving toward Judaism. "The life that was breathed into me, I can't discount," she says.

But Jesus is not part of Judaism. Meredith is not ready to become a Jew, even if she says she wants to become a Jew. You can't be an apple and an orange at the same time. Part of traditional Jewish belief is that all people are created in the image of God and are beloved of God, and that all righteous people, regardless of their creed or religion, have a place in the world to come. There is no need to entice others to our faith. In fact, a tradition exists that would initially discourage those who knock on our door. However, those who persist, who are sincerely motivated to become Jews, are to be welcomed with open arms. Guided by this tradition, I advise Meredith that she shouldn't push herself where she is unwilling to go. But she won't let herself turn back or let me turn her away.

For her upcoming wedding, Meredith wants to be

*married under the huppah (Jewish wedding canopy)
by a rabbi in a Jewish ceremony, even though she also
feels it would be hypocritical to do so. She is genuinely
conflicted, swimming in this sea where the more she
learns, the more she questions. I admire her for her
honesty and for wanting to do the right thing.*

*What has happened is that Allen has started to read
her books. Meredith is giving him access to his heritage, his roots, and he is enjoying it. And she is giving
Allen's seven-year-old daughter some Jewish values.
Together they made a Tzedakah box (to collect money
for charity), and the little girl can't wait to attend her
weekly class at the Jewish Community Center.
Meredith and Allen just upgraded their membership
at the center, and Allen, on his own initiative, signed
up to volunteer for house-painting for the needy.
Never before has he done anything like that with a
Jewish organization.*

*Recently we attended a seminar at the White House
concerning outreach to the Jewish community worldwide. The woman who gave the presentation was a
very charismatic and intellectually stimulating
speaker. Meredith asked whether her mother was
proud of her for the work she was doing. She prefaced
her question by remarking that she really must "feel*

*Jewish" now, because never would she have asked that
question as a Catholic.*

*Only time will tell what Meredith decides to do.
Although she is not a convert, I include her story
because it sheds light on a sensitive subject. If she eventually does convert, it will be only because she accepts
the tenets of Judaism fully. The wrestling she is expe-
riencing will be over, and she will be at peace. When
and if that day comes, Meredith will be an incredible
asset to the Jewish people. But for Meredith right now,
it is not the destination that we are looking at; it's the
road she is traveling.*

Meredith Speaks

I was walking along the street one night. Allen was
in a bookstore, and he looked out the window and
saw me. I had on this big old gray coat. He followed
me down into the subway to get a better look. Then
he bought a fare card and approached me on the plat-
form. He said, "You'll think I'm crazy, but life is too
short—someone passes you on the street who could
be *the one*." Of course I thought he was completely
nuts, but there was nothing smarmy about him. He

was just a guy making a move. I had a boyfriend at the time, so I gave him my business card (I'm a reporter), thinking of him for my single friends. But then he pursued me at work. He scared me because I suspected he was an operator, but we had a lot of things in common. We definitely clicked; there was a connection that wasn't just peripheral.

A Jewish lawyer, Allen grew up in the Midwest where he was always told he was the best at everything. He was the first man I ever met who grew up being pushed intellectually. A graduate of Northwestern and the University of Michigan Law School, he was raised to shoot for the highest; I was not, however. My mother could never quite understand me. She used to rip books out of my hands, say it wasn't normal to want to read all the time and tell me to go outside and play. But I didn't want to go out and play. That's partly why Judaism strikes a chord with me and feels so comfortable. The values that were reinforced for Allen were the ones I always wanted reinforced for me. I see Judaism as fulfilling the striving for perfection that I did not find in my own background.

Allen has been divorced for five years from a gentile woman. During their wedding ceremony, the Christian references alienated him. She had been concerned that he would not go to heaven because he was a Jew, which made him feel uncomfortable. Their values and beliefs were different, but they have a young child together, a little girl.

Meanwhile, I was dating only Catholic boys, mostly from ethnic backgrounds, though I never felt a connection with anyone in a spiritual sense until I met Allen. There had been little religious diversity in the Pittsburgh neighborhood where I grew up, and I had always assumed I needed to find a nice Catholic boy who would share my values. After attending a Catholic university, I received a master's degree in public policy from American University, and then I worked as a reporter for ten years. I entered journalism because I recognized that I am a searcher, and that advocacy can make a difference in this world.

Allen and I knew each other for nine months before we started dating, and we didn't talk about religion for a long time. He was at the point where he had no real desire to explore his religion or culture, so I talked about it before he did. Now we have been together for three years. Had I not met Allen, I would have delayed or not pursued the study of Judaism. Meeting him precipitated it. I'm sensitive about this like many others involved in interfaith relationships;

I'm not exploring Judaism *for* Allen; Allen was not the start of the path, but he was along the path. My love for him makes me want to understand him more. What I was attracted to about Allen is very tied to my interest in Judaism. So I felt that I had no choice but to study with Rabbi Weiss. It was like the choice, the connection, was made for me. I couldn't stop.

I grew up in a working-class Catholic Eastern European neighborhood. That's all I knew. But when I was young, we would drive through the Jewish section of Pittsburgh on Saturday mornings to get bagels, and I remember seeing all these families walking from the synagogue. Here we would go into this other world and see families that seemed very unlike ours. Our church was very staid, very proper; people would show up in all their finery, and whole families didn't go together—at least that was my experience. So to see whole families walking along the street and laughing together, groups of people, I thought, *Who are they?* I was curious. I asked my father why they were coming from church on Saturday, and he answered that not everybody goes to church on Sunday, that their holy day is Saturday, and I remember thinking, *Wow!*

My religious experience growing up was not a traditional straight line; it was more blurred at the

edges. Unlike a lot of the families in our neighborhood who were strict Catholics as far back as they
could remember, we knew we were a combination of
things. My father was Greek Orthodox, though he
would follow Roman Catholicism. But in times of
trouble—there were traumas in the marriage—he
would find comfort in the Greek Orthodox church in
our town. And my mother's great-great-grandparents
were Jewish—from Alsace Lorraine—and they converted to Catholicism. I remember hearing it; it was
part of family lore. So at a young age I learned that
Jews were persecuted, that my own family members
had to leave their religion to escape persecution. I
would not call it a cloud hanging over Judaism, but
rather an obstacle in its way. Who would choose to be
persecuted?

At the same time, my family life was difficult; our
very Catholic hometown had its own brand of persecution. There was a lot of judgment about belonging
to the right parish, a whole food chain of class structure and segregation by parish. Both my parents were
very vocal around the dinner table about that. So in a
way they bred the questioning about the religion in
which we were raised. My mother instilled in me a
real sense of belief and faith, a sense of God and a
connection between mortality and immortality. But

she wasn't doctrinaire; she's a maverick. I was the fourth of six children, the experimental baby, they called me, who was taught to read at age four. In first grade I was sent home from Catholic school because my skirt was too short. I was eating cookies and milk at the table when my mother said, "You're not changing the dress. I'm taking you back!" She pulled us out of Catholic school in third grade because she didn't like what we were being taught. She was very bitter about that. Public school was not so homogenous; there we were getting mixed up with some Protestants.

In fifth-grade catechism class I remember having an argument with the teacher, a former nun, over the symbolism of the Garden of Eden. I remember thinking it was not to be taken literally, that it was a tale like Aesop's fables, there to teach us a lesson. The teacher decided I was a negative influence in the class and needed private tutoring because I was disturbing the other children. That was another thing that made me question my own religion—the inequities and the judgment. The bottom line was that you couldn't question. But my mother did encourage me to dissect doctrine and to question. She follows the spirit of the faith, but not the rules and regulations.

My mother had troubles with my father; they were very ill-suited to each other, yet they had six children together. At age twelve or thirteen, I became aware that she was seeking help from a priest as to whether she should stay in the marriage. Three priests (the trinity, she likes to say, in a funny way) told her that she had to try harder, that *she* was the problem, that she had to stay in the marriage. When I was fifteen, however, my parents got divorced. A long time ago, she said that religion gets in the way of faith. You don't tell your children this without planting some seeds. The best part of my religion was the shared ritual and traditions that really did pave the way for my faith, my belief, my value system. But the trappings of the religion I really never felt at home with. I know that now. I made a distinction early on that there was a God and then there was what man encased God in. I remember that there was a chasm between the way I felt about God and what I was told about God.

Recently I went to an Orthodox Jewish synagogue, and it was one of the most spiritual experiences of my life, just being around true believers. I felt unworthy—that's the reverence I felt. What is so unsettling is that I recognize that I have found not just a faith, but a peace and a sense of home in

Judaism. Judaism feels more right to me than Christianity. I feel I'm just beginning to uncover and peel off all this varnish. At this point I can't turn back. But I'm really torn. It's not the same as going into a store and deciding to change your look with a new outfit. Embracing Judaism is not a makeover. I don't know if I can convert. Yet the more I learn, the more I see and feel and understand and study, Judaism seems much more centered to me than my religious upbringing, which I always questioned and doubted and over which I felt very guilty. Judaism doesn't feel alien to me; it feels comfortable. But in saying that, I'm very hesitant; I'm even nervous in saying that. In a sense I feel like I will always be an outcast no matter what religion I anchor myself in. I'm a hybrid. I never felt like I belonged. But I see my identity tied culturally to the values I was raised in, the values of Catholicism, both good and bad. A part of me feels unworthy to share an experience that I haven't known, I mean the collective experience, the history of the Jews.

I read *The Rise and Fall of the Third Reich* when I was twelve. It was the reason why I wanted to become a journalist. It opened my eyes. I said, "This is real? This happened?" If I had been there, I would have exposed it. I have to write, to document injustice. I remember clearly thinking that. This feeling has led me to where I am now, and it's a feeling that I'm not turning away from. I remember having conversations with my father about it. At eighteen or nineteen he was part of the occupation in Germany after the clean-up. He used to tell stories about camp survivors he met. There was one woman who was beautiful and very fragile, he said, but her eyes were dead, because she had seen everything she loved die. And she was young. Your parents' experiences shape you.

Allen and I went to Poland and Hungary last year and I got very, very upset when we were in Poland. I looked for anti-Semitism; I watched the way people looked at us. Allen laughs at me because I thought everybody was a Jew-hater and everybody was slighting Allen. I remember we took a train from Budapest to Krakow, and I cried the whole night because all I could think was that these were the tracks that would have taken Allen to his death had he been born fifty years earlier in this country. To choose the Jewish life is not to choose the easy road. Allen is the person I love, and I saw Poland and the train tracks in a deeper way. I harbor a lot of unnecessary fears.

My mother's gift to me, all she could give me really, was the values embodied in the religion she gave me. But she knows I'm studying Judaism, and that I want to raise my children as Jews. She has made comments to me like, "Are you going to forget about Christ?" This is what I say to her, and what I tell Allen: "My God is Allen's God. It's the same God." But obviously I'm not totally convinced, or I wouldn't be having this dilemma. Christ was a guide, loving and mortal, and that human element of God is a powerful force. I still struggle with the idea of giving up the belief that Jesus is God, that God and Christ are one and the same. I struggle and straddle the line; I believe Christ is like a representation of God's children, a righteous man—the righteousness part makes you part of God. There are profound questions that I cannot settle in six months of study.

In his way Allen is also reading and studying. If I leave a book open, he reads it. It's a wonderful component of our relationship, exploring Judaism together. But I'm very cynical, very judgmental, of those who convert to please a spouse.

The funny thing is, I have so much to contribute to Judaism. What I bring is about commitment; it's a leap of faith, stepping into the abyss and knowing you won't sink. Allen's daughter and I do projects about Jewish history. She's curious about it, although she is partially being raised by Christian grandparents. In her seven-year-old mind, there's a desire to explore the identity that her father gave her. She's like the coffee additive, half-and-half.

Here's the dilemma: I want my own children to be born Jewish and not to a Christian woman. I don't want to be in a fake Jewish wedding; that would make me feel like a fraud. I don't want to be a faceless, voiceless member of the Jewish community, but a contributor; I want to embrace it wholeheartedly. I feel tied—willingly tethered—to Judaism, something I never felt about Catholicism. At the same time, I feel like I have to defend Christ—I feel defensive about Christ.

I haven't had this experience in my life before—facing something so significant as Judaism, yet being unable to commit to it. I hesitate to predict where I'll be in six months. I know I want my children, our children, to be Jewish even if I'm not. I want to give them a gift of history and survival and life embodied in a religion that has persevered despite every attempt to squash it. I don't want Allen's Judaism to die out with Allen. I want to perpetuate it. I want a foundation to build a future. I don't want him to get lost in an interfaith marriage. Maybe the world has enough Christians.

When I see self-loathing in Jews, I want to say to them that I thought I could never identify with being a Jew because I could never identify with victimization. But that was mainstream history's projection on Jews. The Torah is about life and endurance and survival. When I see a Jew with self-loathing, I think, You're out of touch with the teachings of your religion.

My religious path has brought me to a place where there are no easy decisions. God's existence I've never really questioned. I have seen and felt God in my life and I know that I cannot live without God or religion. I feel that I'm following the right way. But I don't know where it's leading me.

Meredith's Thoughts on Some Elements of Faith

The Search for God

I've searched for some evidence that God exists beyond written parables of a garden where a snake could corrupt and a land where deliverance from slavery was handed over by a touch of a staff and the parting of a sea. The power of faith, of belief, must be grounded by more than fantastic tales of magic, anchored by more than the hope embodied in such allegories. That is what I tell myself. That is why I search.

And so I search like an archeologist reconstructing

an ancient world, where a shard of broken pottery can be expanded into a holy vessel, a cryptic message can be deciphered into a universal truth. But unlike other intellectual journeys, faith cannot be found this way, I sense. God cannot be unearthed, found. And yet I have felt God, I have seen God act in my own and others' lives. I have witnessed the reality of God's existence, but I can offer no concrete evidence of it. God merely is—I am as certain of that as I am of the sun's reappearance each day, unaided by man's intervention. Like my beating heart, my crowded thoughts, which exist separate and yet in sum of me—unaided by religious teaching.

When Disaster Strikes

A faith built on ritual and tradition is more likely to sustain a lifetime of loss and disappointment and brief moments of joy. When disaster strikes, cling to the familiar comfort. Religion centers us, defines our identity, shelters us in community and the collective awe of the unknown hand guiding our lives and meting out an impenetrable justice.

Scholarship Has Its Place in Religion

Scholarship has its place in religion. But access to it must be through the hands of something more, someone who understands, who feels, who allows, who accommodates. Like Rabbi Weiss.

Visiting Auschwitz

People would picnic on the outside grounds while death was going on inside the barbed wires. It was dumb luck; the evidence of evil clogs your throat. The identity of the Jews was stolen in Eastern Europe. Their identity was killed, but no one would help them. The people that worked in the camps, the faces I saw, reach the part of you that has no speech, you are so vulnerable. It is the non-Jews we have to save. They have revised history to fit their conscience.

Conversion

I think of conversion as the great unwashed dipping into the waters of who you are and turning into the person that you want to become.

Rosh Hashanah and Yom Kippur

Ten days of dreaming about sins gives one the opportunity to change. Yom Kippur is when one empties the pockets in order to fill them again.

TEN

Finding a New Me

Ezra's Rebirth

Unlike the young men and women whom you've already met in these pages, Ezra is not a Christian marrying a Jew, or already married to a Jew. He sought me out for different reasons, but I include his story because many of the issues that concerned him are universal and should appeal to both Jews and those contemplating entering the family of Judaism.

When Ezra first came to me, he was lost, grasping for something. He had the air of a drifter, so unsure was he of himself and of the direction his life was taking. Nervous and unhappy, he was looking for something, but he didn't know what—something to hold on to that would give meaning and purpose to his existence.

Ezra was raised as an island in time, neither here nor there. His mother was Christian and his father was a Jew by birth only. Ezra couldn't walk into a church because he didn't feel at home; nor could he walk into a synagogue because he didn't feel at home there, either. He came to me as a twenty-three-year-old adult. His love for his Jewish grandmother had spurred him to learn something about her background. Over the course of a year, we studied together. Ezra began to embrace the Jewish tradition and culture. Eventually, he went through a Conservative Jewish conversion, followed by a Bar Mitzvah in a Conservative synagogue. Yet he always gravitated to a nearby Orthodox synagogue. I put him in contact with a young Orthodox couple who invited him for Shabbat dinners. Then I lost touch with Ezra.

While I was away in Israel on a Melton Fellowship at Hebrew University in Jerusalem, Ezra became much more Orthodox in his observance. He began wearing tzitzis (the fringes of the prayer shawl) hanging outside his clothing like many Orthodox men and associating himself with the Orthodox community. When he was my student, Ezra would give me a warm hug and a kiss, but when I saw him recently, like many very Orthodox men, he avoided touching me. Such was the manifestation of the new way of life that he had chosen.

He was introduced to a young woman from an Orthodox background with whom he fell in love. Now they are engaged and soon to be married. At an engagement party I attended, the room was filled with Orthodox men in black hats and Orthodox women wearing sheitels (wigs) and long dresses. The smile on Ezra's face was warm and welcoming, and he had a special air about him that I hadn't seen before, an air of contentment and serenity, coupled with happiness and joy. Here at last he belonged.

Ezra gave a speech analyzing that week's portion of the Torah that demonstrated such a knowledge of the Bible and Talmud that I was simply over-whelmed. He had come such a long way. It is hard to describe my feelings when I saw how comfortable he felt talking in front of this very Orthodox crowd. As I was getting ready to leave, he and his bride-to-be asked me to be a matron of honor in their wedding.

Coming Out of the Desert with a Shofar in My Hands

I grew up in Vienna, Virginia. My dad is Jewish; my mother is not. We had a Christmas tree, though my mom, a lapsed Lutheran, never went to church, and is more of an agnostic. We didn't really have a relationship with my mother's side of the family. She comes from a different world, from a family of farmers and lumberjacks, original pioneer settlers in the West. Her marrying a Jew contributed to her estrangement from them, since it presented a situation outside their limited experience. Yet the only thing Jewish we ever did was light Chanukah candles and attend a Passover seder every year at the home of family friends.

I always wanted to have more involvement with that world, however, and looked forward to Passover. I gravitated toward it. I wanted more, in fact. I had always sort of missed having a Bar Mitzvah. On the other hand, at Christmas I was just white-knuckled. It felt alien. I never liked it. There were so many paradoxes that didn't make sense to me, and the behavior of Christians in the world was not positive. There were clear contradictions. Some taboos seemed to me not realistic and to negate human nature.

I grew up involved in music (guitar) and studied at a conservatory and at the University of North Texas. In college I was attracted to New Age meditating—I suppose because it was packaged so well, as something more in touch with today than older religious mysticism. One day I was quieting my mind, doing the meditations. Then out of nowhere something was telling me that I'm not alone in my mind here, that my consciousness was affected by some kind of outside source in the universe, an idea or a communication. I don't usually believe in these paranormal experiences, but this was definitely one of them. I felt I was being communicated to. It proved to me that, yes, there is something out there.

An epiphany of sorts? Well, I don't think I'm worthy of that specific word, but it was a feeling I would describe as warm, blissful, happy. Your mind has to be still so you can accept any kind of communication with the universe. It has never really happened again to me since then. I've had other moments, at the Wailing Wall in Jerusalem, and sometimes just davening (praying). But that first time was the message. So it made me ask myself, Now what? It got me started on the road back to where I am. I decided to become more involved with Judaism—even the Hindus tell you to practice in the way you know—but I was at a loss as to what to do.

Passover was coming up and I thought to myself, *I cannot* not *have Passover, especially now. I really need it.* At the time I had just flopped as a musician, was dirt poor, and had nothing else going for me. I was reading a paper, trying to find a bass player to put a band together, when I spotted Rabbi Weiss's announcement for an adult-education class in Judaism. I called her up and told her my story. Then she invited me for Passover. It felt good, and Rabbi Weiss thought I was brave to come without knowing anybody. I went through a year-long study program and decided to go the whole nine yards and have a Conservative conversion. But already I was moving toward the Orthodox tradition. The Orthodox synagogue was the only place I felt at home; to me, there was a feeling of community that the Conservative and Reform were missing. I knew that within the Orthodox community was where I wanted to be. Yet I still wasn't a fully practicing Jew; it took another year of study and practice before my Orthodox conversion.

At the time, I had basically been unemployed and was barely supporting myself by teaching private music lessons. I had studied at one of the most prestigious music schools in the world, and I didn't think it was fair. It was frustrating, depressing; at twenty-five I felt like I was behind the game. But as I continued to study Judaism, my whole life started to come together. I was rebuilding, getting some order into my life. I now play guitar only semi-professionally. My main occupation is running a computer network for a nonprofit organization. The computer, like music, involves abstract thinking, so there seems to be a link there as to my abilities.

An Orthodox friend introduced me to my wife-to-be. He invited both of us to Shabbos (Sabbath) dinner but completely blindsided me. I had no idea what he was doing. Immediately I saw real potential in the relationship, and just one week later we were both sure about each other.

My mom really likes and respects Judaism and has been very supportive of my observance. She even studies Judaism to keep up with me and has gone to the trouble of kashering (making kosher) her kitchen in order to make me Thanksgiving dinner. You couldn't ask for more support, really. Likewise, my dad has been very positive, though he was a little nervous when I started hanging out with Orthodox Jews because he wasn't sure how far I would take it. He was afraid I would become fanatic. But I'm pretty centrist Orthodox.

If you overritualize, you can be so caught up in the rules that you forget what they are there for. If you are a convert like me, you have a tremendous advantage. You don't take anything for granted because you approach everything with a critical view.

Now I feel like I'm coming out of the desert with a shofar (ram's horn) in my hands, ready to tear down the walls of Jericho. I feel I'm on the verge of achieving a lot. I've had my first good job for a year now and I'm saving some money. I'm starting a family, and I'm getting back into music. I'm involved in a community with lots of friends whom I love and don't want to leave.

Everything down to meeting my fiancée, I feel, has been engineered. There must be a Director. I took good stuff out of hardship; I pulled the survival spirit out of it, and I wouldn't change the experience because the end result is a very good thing. And my music—there's an emotional content to it, a drive there, in my arranging music. I write for my fiancée. Best of all, I'm happy with my life. I have order, I have shalom (peace).

Ezra's Tips for Converts

1. One of the first things you should learn to do is bench grace (sing grace) after meals and learn a couple of frequently sung songs as well—"L'cha Dodi" ("Come, My Beloved"), for example—so you won't feel awkward at meals and just sit there.
2. While learning in general, try to learn a lot about something specific, become more of an expert in one area so you can contribute to conversation and not feel like a kid.

3. There is a myth that an Orthodox rabbi must reject the convert three times. That's not true. If he does this, find another rabbi. (That never happened to me.)

4. Going home to visit parents can be a problem. Everyone feels awkward. Expect it to be an ordeal and do it anyway.

5. Two of the most helpful books I read are *Kitzur Shulchan Aruch* (Code of Jewish Law) and Zelig Pliskin's *Love Your Neighbor.*

6. Go to Israel. Make no excuses about money or any of that. You must go to Israel.

7. Find peers whom you can relate to who are converts and get to know them as well as families.

8. Don't feel as if you have an obligation to tell people that you're converting, that you're not Jewish by birth. The challenge is to fit in and to not be treated any differently at all. I don't want people to bend over backwards to do anything for me. And I've never seen a convert who is not accepted.

9. Learn from reading, from free classes, from sessions with rabbis, from Talmud classes and from friends. Aryeh Kaplan books are very helpful.

ELEVEN

An African-American Chooses Judaism

The End of Elizabeth's Search

 *Elizabeth, age forty-two, a beautiful and brilliant black lawyer, a Harvard Law School graduate, was born in Raleigh, North Carolina, the only child of Protestant parents. She studied international affairs at Georgetown University, where she met her husband, an Ethiopian Christian, to whom she has been married for eighteen years. She has worked in government, for nonprofit human rights refugee resettlement organizations and as a private consultant.*

Among my students Elizabeth is the exception, that rare individual who comes to Judaism completely on her own, with no Jewish connection, no obvious impetus to delve into it. Like the legendary king of the Khazars in the Middle Ages, Elizabeth decided to embrace Judaism only after making a careful examination of several religions. She went to the

library, she read, she investigated like a scientist, look-
ing for answers that satisfied both her intellectual and
spiritual needs. Judaism made the most sense to her,
more so than other faiths, including the faith of her
youth. She wanted a religion that would be a part of
her everyday life and that she could observe in the
home. She wanted to feel accountable to something
beyond herself. Strictly observant, she finds in
Judaism a purpose, a way, a structure to which she
can cling.

Elizabeth: Sammy Davis and Me

I didn't know anyone both black and Jewish except
for Sammy Davis Jr., whom I had read about in a
magazine, so since I grew up in the South, Judaism
was simply not an option for me. On the television on
Sundays, I always saw the same religion: Christianity.
I had friends in high school who were Jewish, though,
one who kept kosher even, and another who told me
about the Passover seder. But it was the South and we
just never really talked about their religion.

Although we went to church when I was little, I
mostly learned about God at home through Bible

stories. Most significant to me was the story of Joseph. It was astounding to me that a slave could become so important. I felt bad about slavery, and questioned why God had allowed it to happen to black people. Was it something the people had done, I wondered—or was it that God couldn't be concerned with them because they were only insignificant slaves? Since I was descended from slaves, perhaps God was not concerned about me either.

It was such an eye-opener to find that God was indeed concerned about Joseph and about slaves; I feel I got my first real glimpse of God through that story. I asked a lot of questions about it, which laid the foundation for the way I would eventually go. As a young person, I had wanted to have some kind of knowledge of the Bible as literature. But instead of starting with the New Testament, I started at the beginning, with the Hebrew Bible. My thoughts and opinions were thus shaped by what Christians call the Old Testament. When I said my prayers, I always addressed God rather than Jesus. In the back of my mind I could never understand the concept of the trinity. I thought to myself, *This can't be right*. At the same time, you don't want to reject what your parents are teaching you. If I rejected the tradition of my parents, was I disobeying or dishonoring them? I was really confused.

By the time I got to Georgetown University, I was searching for something, for a religious community. It's a Jesuit university, so naturally I looked to Catholicism. But it didn't resonate with me at all. As a foreign exchange student in Latin America, I couldn't handle the icons and statues. Others felt fervently religious, but I felt totally alien. So I decided to let Catholicism go and see what happened as time went on. It just wasn't a good fit. In fact, nothing fit until Judaism entered my life. It seemed to me that Judaism was the only religion out in the world doing things, with an emphasis on community and saving the world. That sounded like something I could be a part of.

After my freshman year of college, I kept religion on a back burner for some time and kept these questions about Christianity in the back of my mind. By the mid-1980s, I was married and employed as an independent consultant, and living in Arlington, Virginia, a suburb of Washington, D.C. I started thinking that I should be involved in a religious community. So I investigated; I shopped around. In the library I looked at the doctrines of different religions. I read the doctrines of the Episcopalians, but no, I couldn't agree with them. I visited the Presbyterian Church; I studied the doctrines of the African

Methodists (AME); I went to Sunday school classes, but I was not satisfied with any of them. They all emphasized the trinity and the incarnation, and there was no way I could accept that. So I came to the conclusion that I shouldn't be a Christian. I felt there must be some group out there that believes in the oneness of God and puts the emphasis on doing the commandments. I guess I was really looking for Judaism all the time, but I didn't know it.

So what about the covenant of Abraham? Could I join? I wondered. An article from the *Washington Post* announced a Torah class at a local Reform synagogue early on Saturday mornings. I inquired and was assured that it would be okay for a non-Jew to attend. I went, and am I glad it was a Reform class because had it been Orthodox, I would have been totally lost. I took my niece with me because I didn't want to go by myself. The people were friendly and I enjoyed the class. I went with the idea of broadening my horizons, of merely seeing what other people were doing. But I found that what I was looking for—what I was saying, what I felt most comfortable with—was there. There was no point in looking any further. I had found it.

I stayed for the prayer services. A woman cantor was singing *Mi Khamokha*. When she sang, suddenly

I knew this was the place I had to be. And when I took the bus home, I felt like a part of me had suddenly awakened. I felt that my intellect had been involved and utilized in worship, not suppressed. I was thinking on that bus that I simply had to go back. I feel that my soul came home that day. I was at ease.

At the same time, I was wondering how I would feel if I went back. There were so many blacks in Washington that I was surprised there were none in the synagogue. I figured there would be more black Jews by choice or blacks whose mothers or fathers were Jewish. Color was not an issue for me, but I worried that others might not be so color-blind. I was concerned that I would stand out. I'm shy and I like to blend, not draw attention to myself. *I want to be there, I need to be there*, I thought to myself, *but will I be comfortable?* Yet the feeling of being at home in the synagogue was so strong that it overcame my reservations, so I went back again to the study group. Particularly because of this experience, I believe there is a God and a purpose to the universe and that God cares about our lives.

A Member of Two Minorities

I subscribed to the *Washington Jewish Week*, joined a few Jewish book clubs and visited the Jewish bookstore frequently. So I was reading, reading, reading. Then I'd bring up some Midrash (Jewish narrative) with my non-Jewish friends and they would say, "You seem to be going more and more Jewish these days; where are you going with this?" But I didn't know. What I was looking for was someone to tell me that it was okay for me to become Jewish, that I would be welcome.

There was a Jewish woman where I had worked in the early 1980s who was very involved with her religion. We had exchanged seasonal cards; this time I wrote her a note explaining that I was studying Judaism but had not yet converted because I was unsure how it would be to be a member of two minorities, to be both black and Jewish. I was fishing for her to say that it wouldn't matter at all, but she didn't do that. So I thought, *Well, maybe this isn't the right moment for such a move.*

Then one day I was having lunch with someone and we were discussing having children. I said, "If I ever have children, I want to raise them as Jews." My friend said she was not surprised. She said, "You want

structure, discipline and something very rational."
No one else had put it quite that way. It was then that
I realized I was going to convert. From that moment
on, whenever something with Jewish content was
held open to the public, I would try to go, whether it
was a seder at a synagogue, or a concert by a Jewish
singer. At one community seder, a Russian Jewish
refusnik was visibly moved by the number of people
attending openly and without fear. He spoke of his
personal exodus from the Soviet Union and how that
experience made the words "in every generation one
must see himself as personally coming out of Egypt"
real for him. His story was so moving; something
inside—a recognition of sorts—just clicked. I said to
myself, "Yes, I too am coming out of Egypt." It was
time for me to take the leap.

I don't remember precisely how I came across
Rabbi Weiss's name, but I called and made an
appointment. I met a number of people taking classes
with her, and I started going with them to different
synagogues. I found the Conservative synagogue in
my neighborhood to be very friendly, and after my
conversion I started attending it regularly. Yet I occasionally attended an Orthodox synagogue as well and
found myself being pulled in that direction. I am still
very attracted to the Orthodox tradition because of

its strong emphasis on halacha (the law), which is very important to me.

At first it didn't bother me much that my husband isn't Jewish (I didn't want to force him), but it does now. I miss the family part of Judaism. I'm not content any more with his religious status, and the more discontent I am, the more it is a problem in the marriage. The Jewish community, Israel and Judaism are so important to me that I find it very unsettling not to share those feelings with my husband. He tries to be supportive, but I would like it better if he would be committed some day, especially if we have a child.

My mother became ill recently, and I have been living with her in Raleigh, North Carolina, and helping her manage the family real estate business. (My husband commutes on weekends.) I redid my mother's kitchen (it needed a face-lift anyway) so that I could observe kashrut (the kosher laws). At first my mother was very surprised by how much work was involved and that I would take the time to do it. But I try to keep kashrut the best I can (I never eat in nonkosher restaurants), and I observe Shabbos and dress modestly. Keeping kosher is one of the ways I'm connected to my identity as a Jew.

In this small area where I reside, far from an established Jewish community, in the house where I grew up, I really want to affirm my Judaism. So the things I can do by myself, I do. I make an extra effort. Had I been born Jewish, I like to think I would be equally observant.

It's funny how I sometimes miss the Orthodox shul I occasionally attended in the Washington area. I get up on Shabbos, and the way the sun comes in the window reminds me of just how the sun filtered through the window of the shul. I don't want to drive on Shabbos, since I never did (I walked to synagogue) and would feel uncomfortable doing that; so attending shul across town in Raleigh would be difficult. In fact, I would be unhappy to drive to shul. Walking on Shabbos became my habit. It was always so pleasurable; it was a very good memory; you would see others walking and you'd stop and talk.

My mother is pleased with my becoming a Jew. She is totally happy with it because she feels I have finally got something. She comes to Shabbos dinner and is ecstatic because she thinks it is so beautiful. I shared my feelings and thoughts with her while I studied for conversion, and she was very supportive and quite excited for me. I didn't tell my father because I didn't want to hurt him. I thought he would interpret my decision not only as a rejection of his faith, but also of him personally. My mother recently told me that she had discussed my conversion with my father and that he had accepted it. I'm glad he knew of my conversion before his death, and, more important, that my decision caused him no pain.

In the future I see myself becoming more involved with Jewish organizations, such as volunteers for Israel, maybe studying there, and doing grassroots work within Jewish organizations that help people. Judaism is about taking what you've learned and putting it into practice to make a difference in someone's life. The little things we do may have a big effect. As to conflicts between blacks and Jews, it's painful for me to read about them, but I think anti-Jewish statements by some blacks get a lot more attention in the media than they do among black people themselves. I keep myself apart from these conflicts and always try to bridge gaps.

There's the traditional saying, if someone converts it's as if he or she has always been Jewish. I feel I have a Jewish soul. Since I was little I was in a constant struggle to understand God and where I fit in the universe. I didn't just accept what was given to me; I was always questioning and trying to understand. Now I feel at peace.

TWELVE

"The Last Person to Date a Jew"

Susan and Rob's Transformation

When Susan first came to me upon the recommendation of friends, she had already made a decision to convert to Judaism, the religion of her fiancé, Rob. But making that a reality seemed beyond her grasp. Work for a big telecommunications network required that Susan spend part of her time in Mexico and part of her time in California. The possibility of taking classes in Judaism had been out of the question because of her hectic schedule, she said.

I felt Susan was very smart because she knew how important Judaism was for Rob even if he wasn't especially observant. (He grew up in a family deeply committed to Judaism.) She really loves him and will do whatever it takes to make the relationship work. Susan asked if I could figure a way to help them.

We met at a Chanukah party I was having for my

145

students in my home. Susan struck me as a very spiritual person. Religion was important to her—belief in God and letting religious practice be a part of her life. Some people don't care much about religion, but Susan did. In the past she had gone to church weekly, but "it had never really clicked" for her, she told me. Susan left armed with books and assignments and a lot of information in her head. Together we planned a year-long program that was suitable to her schedule, but it would take a tremendous effort on her part to see it through. Wherever she was, she would have to call me on a weekly basis for an hourly lesson. Most people would have thought this idea was crazy, absurd (most people did when she told them about it), but I knew it would work for Susan.

I was impressed with Susan's responsiveness, her commitment to her studies, the way she kept to her word. She called from Mexico, from San Diego, from Washington, D.C. It took a lot of coordinating, but I could always count on her. She could have decided that it was just too much of an effort, but she didn't. She did her assignments, and she and Rob went to services together (she found the places to go). I admire her for that. I have no doubt about her sincerity. The investment of her time is the indicator of her commitment.

I met with her a few months ago to ground her and give her my support for what she is doing. That was part of the arrangement we had, that we would meet together several times a year. I will see her again just before she goes before the Bet Din for conversion. It's important because she is more nervous than a student who meets with me all the time.

Susan is a very intelligent person, with a strong personality. She is devoted to her family and to her job. I think she will be a good Jew and will bring Rob back to Judaism. She has already made a New Year's resolution that they will attend synagogue together at least once a month. Susan often goes to his parents' home on Friday nights, and she does the blessings. Rob's parents are thrilled with this. It wasn't hard for her to make the transition to Judaism. In fact, it turns out she has found the vehicle for her religious expression. Susan is a leader; she makes things happen, and she'll be a star in her synagogue some day.

Susan: "The Last Person to Date a Jew"

When I first met Rob I honestly didn't know he was Jewish. I had no idea. We had been friends at work. So I said to him at a happy hour after work one day, "What are you doing for Christmas?" He said, "Nothing; I'm Jewish." It took him a year to bring religion up again. His grandmother encouraged him.

When I told my friend from college, who is Jewish, about Rob and about my becoming a Jew, she said, "You're about the last person I would expect to ever date a Jew." She knows that I didn't grow up around any Jewish people. In the small town in central Pennsylvania where I lived, my entire school was white Protestant and Catholic. I probably had no thoughts about Jews at all. I didn't even know any Jewish people until I met my friend in college. Even the jokes were Polish or Italian jokes, not Jewish.

When I realized I cared a great deal for Rob, on my own I bought the book *To Be a Jew*. I just asked my friend for a suggestion for an overview. I knew being Jewish was an important part of Rob's life; exploring Judaism was just a way of getting to know him better. I said to Rob about a year ago, when we first started talking about religion, "Well, if you're going to ask me to consider Judaism, would you consider my religion?" I'm trying to remember exactly what he said. He said it would be highly unlikely that he would ever convert to my faith. I felt I had to ask this question, even though I already knew the answer I would get. It has to do with the desire to preserve the Jewish people. It's very important to Rob's family that he carry on the Jewish tradition. I kind of shrugged my question off. If I had pressed Rob on it, I doubt we would be where we are today. I simply asked the question, got the answer and moved beyond it.

Religion is important enough to both of us that we are not going to have no religion in our life together as a couple and as a family. We talked about it a lot; we made the decision to have one religion instead of two. If you maintain both, saying a child can choose, they wind up with nothing. I want my children to have a religious background. I have friends who don't have that, and I think they are missing out on a major portion of life.

Meeting Rob was . . . it was right. I had some boyfriends in the past, but my previous relationships always seemed like work. We didn't really get along. I was crying; I was upset. Then Rob came along. It's the old cliché: You'll know when it's right—and you do! I can't say it was love at first sight—and I think Rob would say the same thing—but our relationship just flows. It's easy; we get along so well. The best part is, we balance one another. I'm the high-strung one, he's the easygoing one. So we reached that moment when you know this is the one you want to spend your life with. I made the decision to become a Jew; this is the path I chose to pursue. I feel like I'm converting not for Rob, but for us, for our future family. I felt it would take a toll on our relationship if I didn't. He would be very disappointed. This means a lot to him, I know it. He's very appreciative and supportive.

Together we will decide to what degree we will follow this way of life. I would like to have children right away. But it's up to God. There's no guarantee that's going to happen. But we know we're going to raise them Jewish, with many of the traditions. Just because you don't observe every single law of Judaism, that doesn't take away from your being Jewish.

I was religious, but never ultrareligious, as a Protestant. I never believed Jesus was God, just the son of God. I always prayed to God, never to Jesus Christ. I don't know if that was unusual or not, or considered right or wrong. In Judaism, Jesus is a man with no more important a role than anyone else. That theological aspect is not a problem for me. But studying Judaism has been a journey that causes me to think and to ask questions. The question I had over and over was: How do I stop believing in something that I've believed in for thirty years? The answer that I got from within myself was: It's like everything else; it just takes time. With time, you grow into it. I'll definitely never forget what I was taught earlier, but I've learned the differences between the two faiths, and I've made the choice to follow Judaism. I was kind of struggling with it at the beginning. I'm sure every convert does. I had a discussion with my girlfriend (she's Jewish); I said, "I feel like I'm losing my roots." She said, "You're not losing them; you're just repotting them." You know, that's true. That's how I feel. You spend over thirty years believing one way, and then you make this change. It's not something you take lightly. You don't wake up one morning and say, I'm going to be Jewish today. It requires thought and decisions.

I don't have feelings of guilt about leaving Christianity behind, but rather feelings that I'll miss it. Getting ready for the Christmas holidays is fun. It's family tradition; it's what I grew up with—like decorating my home. I'll miss it. But it's something that over time I'm sure I'll miss less and less. As Rob and I start our life together, we will develop our own family traditions. You look on the positive side. This is a new experience like many others in life. Some resist change; others accept it. I have grown from it. I have more of a religious knowledge than ever before. I never sat around and read the Bible before. I may have had it as a goal; I just never got there.

It's a big decision to become a Jew. I looked at Judaism as a religion previously, but now I have come to understand that while it's still a religion, it's also a way of life. There were times in the beginning, when I was working down in Mexico, and I was reading, reading, reading all kinds of Jewish books. I thought to myself: I can read my entire life, but only when I become active in Judaism—attending synagogue, practicing the holiday traditions—will my comfort level be helped. I don't fully think of myself as a Jew yet. I'd say I'm in limbo right now, like the man without a country. I think when I formally convert it will really hit home.

When I'm with Rob's family for Shabbat, they always make me feel welcome. Sometimes when we're in synagogue, though, I kind of wonder if people know I'm not Jewish yet, that I haven't converted yet. When I'm there, I'm more apt to say "Hi," not "Shalom." That kind of thing might give me away. But I think I'll feel differently when I go through the conversion process.

Rob is the family favorite. He's kind, caring, very reliable, very responsible. His oldest brother is an

Orthodox rabbi in Israel; they have respect for one another's opinions. His brother was not happy with Rob's choice of a convert because the family is "Kohanim"—members of the priestly class. Under Orthodox law a Kohen cannot marry a convert. This presented some personal baggage that Rob had to work through and resolve on his own. His parents are modern Orthodox, so I don't know how they felt about this issue initially. Maybe marrying a convert wasn't the ultimate dream that every Jewish family has for their son, but because I'm making the effort to convert, they're caring and understanding and willing to meet me halfway. Rob is happy and they are genuinely happy for both of us.

My sister (we're very close) and my mom (my father passed away eight years ago) were very supportive of my choice to become a Jew. "You've always made good decisions, and I've always respected your decisions," my mom said. They asked questions to help them understand my new faith. My mom even went out and purchased a book about Judaism. She is happy as long as I have a belief. She would be bothered if I didn't have any kind of religious affiliation. I know how important this conversion is to Rob and his family, but I don't ever want my family to feel they come in second. He's very understanding about that. I don't think it will ever be a big problem. I'll have to explain to my children some day why their cousins have a Christmas tree and they don't. But I think we'll be able to work through it when the time comes.

Maybe I'm making it seem easier than it is, but in California, it's not as segregated as things used to be where I grew up in central Pennsylvania. When people hear I'm converting, they will ask questions out of curiosity—or ignorance. Questions like, "Can you still come to our Christmas party?" My boss and my close coworkers are saying, "Oh, that's kind of cool." I guess I'm really lucky. In fact, I feel like Rob and I have been very blessed. It seems like everything is going so well. You get engaged, you buy a new home, your jobs are going well. Sometimes you wonder, *Is something bad going to happen?* I just pray that it's not. I just try to relax and enjoy these good times.

I think if my dad were still alive, I would have had a tougher time with it because he was set in his ways. He lived within five miles of where he was born his entire life—that was all he ever wanted to do. That was his personality with everything. He thought it was crazy—that I was nuts—to move to California. He wasn't into big changes. Recently Rabbi Weiss asked me to pick my Hebrew name. I thought about it and decided to choose the name Rebecca, with my dad in mind. He always wanted a "Rebecca," but when my mom was in labor and a lot of pain, she won out with the names she wanted. Now my father will have his wish. He'll have his Rebecca.

So my only questions are internal ones. I think God wants me to do this, though I'm sure when Christmas rolls around I'll definitely have thoughts about the path I've chosen—but more from the tradition point of view, the family holiday aspect, than from the religious part. I will probably go to church with my family. Rob has no problem with that. The way I look at it, it's one hour of my life, and if it's one hour that will make my mom happy, then that's what I'll do. When children come along, Rob and I will just have to figure out a way to integrate it.

I'm identifying more as a Jew every day. If there's something in the news about Israel, I pay much more attention to it now than I did five years ago. I'm much more aware of Judaism and Jews around me—whether reading about it in the paper or just knowing when the holidays are. It comes from studying and attending synagogue. But it's still going to take more time until I can say, "I'm Jewish." Sometimes I think I'm as ready as I'm ever going to be. I don't know if

I'm ever going to wake up and think, *This is the day*. It's more like, you know you want to do this and the reasons why you do it, and you do it. Maybe it's like having kids. Are you ever ready to be the perfect parent? Are you ever ready to be the perfect Jew? The most pleasant surprise for me is that Judaism is a religion that is constantly being studied; being Jewish is an ongoing learning process. I'm sure Rob went to Hebrew school, but my studying Judaism has revitalized things in him that he has forgotten; he has a renewed appreciation of Judaism.

Just now I'm feeling anxious about becoming a Jew. I've spent months and months in preparation—it takes a lot of time—and I'm ready to get on to the next phase of my life. There's such anticipation. The day of my conversion I'll be nervous, but I know when the day comes, I'll be ready. It's a scary thought that you're joining a minority that is sometimes subject to hate crimes. I asked Rob if he had ever been victimized or felt any prejudice directed toward him. He said no, not really. He also said he doesn't hide being Jewish, but he doesn't publicize it either. If someone meets him, he doesn't say, "Hi, I'm Rob and I'm a Jew." It's crossed my mind that even in San Diego there have been different anti-Semitic incidents. In the movie *Life Is Beautiful*, the wife, even though she is not Jewish, insists on going with her husband and son to the concentration camp. When Rob and I walked out of the theater, my heart was broken. I said I would have done the same thing she did. I meant it, too, and not just for the child, but for Rob.

Rob Speaks: "Now I'm at Ease in My Heart"

I always thought I would marry someone Jewish, even though I never dated many Jewish women. I didn't consciously limit myself; I always felt it was far enough away that it didn't matter. I knew dating Susan was different, but I didn't know how far it would progress. It slowly developed into something special. After a year I knew we had to address the religion issue. It was time to have a talk about the future. We had a couple of conversations about wanting our kids to have a unified religious background, not a mixed marriage. It turns out I was more interested in preserving my Jewish heritage, and she was more interested in looking into Judaism, than I was in moving away from being Jewish. I think partly Susan is doing this for me and partly she is doing it because she wants a unified religious practice for her family. She is more willing to compromise that way than I was.

I view Judaism as a strong piece of my family bond. If I were to leave it, I would lose part of that bond. It would hurt my family. They probably would have accepted it over time, but it would have hurt my relationship with my older brother and others. My family has the view of trying to preserve Jewishness through the generations. Susan's converting helps assure that. It's an important value of theirs—and of mine as well. Judaism is a special way of life, a heritage and practice. I'm not religious in terms of going to synagogue all the time, but I feel spiritually linked to Judaism and to Jews. I believe in God as something from within, not a Supreme Being, but something spiritual from within. When Susan and I were talking about our views of God and spirituality, we found that even though we came from different religious traditions, we weren't very far apart in our points of view. I think Susan found she could find spirituality within Judaism. That's why it was easier for her to embrace my religion.

One of the most important things for me, as I moved forward with Susan, was that I didn't want to sever family relationships. I spoke to my grandmother first to find out how my family would feel about my marrying a convert to Judaism. At first my grandmother was overjoyed that I had found someone important enough to me that I had the need to ask those kinds of questions. Her point of view was, if you feel you're doing the right thing, go for it. I felt positive after speaking with her. She's the matriarch of the family. I felt empowered. I thought she would respond that way, but I was also looking for some confirmation. I wrote a letter to my parents and to my older brother after that. At some point I became aware that Orthodox Judaism doesn't allow Kohanim (the priestly class) to marry converts. I'm a Kohen. This became a soul-searching thing for me because my brother and my parents are Orthodox. I had believed in my heart that it was fine to marry a convert, so this was the first time I felt I might be doing something against protocol. I did some research. In the Conservative and Reform traditions, a member of the priestly class marrying a convert isn't an issue. I had to decide who I was. After I talked it over with Rabbi Weiss, I felt my Jewishness was based on the Conservative point of view. That's how I was raised as a child. Internally I resolved it that way.

My parents accepted my decision. My parents' primary thoughts on our relationship were that I find somebody whom I could love and who loves me, and that we could grow together. My Orthodox brother didn't approve of my decision from the religious angle—but he thought Susan's converting was a good thing. Without condoning it, I think he understands what I'm doing and that it has merit over other options we could have taken. That was important for me to hear. Now I'm at ease in my heart and I'm going forward with no reservations.

A Grandmother's Reaction

Rob came from California to Florida to spend the weekend with me last year. He didn't tell me why he was coming, but I'm eighty-five years old and six of my grandsons have come to me about their love affairs. He brought me a beautiful gift and we had a wonderful weekend. I knew he was seeing Susan. Indirectly he would bring up her name in conversation. He had never been serious with anybody before. I knew Susan wasn't Jewish, but most, if not all, of his Jewish friends were married to non-Jews. If we didn't approve of his choice, he might break away from the family. I felt I didn't want to lose him—he's such a wonderful young man. I wanted to hear his side of the story. My daughter (his mother) knew he was coming, but I never told her the conversation we had. I kept it in confidence. He wanted to break it to me himself—he didn't want anybody else to tell me.

I'm an active member of my synagogue and spend my time raising money for Hadassah (a worldwide Jewish women's organization). I observe the Sabbath and celebrate the holidays. My children were brought up in a Jewish home. All three of my daughters keep kosher homes, and I have two grandsons who are very Orthodox. One is a rabbi. I thank God a thousand times a day for my family. Every other phrase out of my mouth is, thank you God. Judaism is important to me, and I would much prefer that my grandchildren marry Jews because then their children will be brought up as Jews. I know Rob would like a Jewish home and family too. He's crazy about his mother and father; he respects his brother; he's a family man, Rob is. I don't think he would hurt his mother and father; it's part of his value system.

He talked to me about Susan and about her job. He listened to everything I had to say (I talked and talked), and I realized at that moment that if Susan made him happy, that was all right with me. If she made him happy, then I was happy. I wasn't going to lose him under any condition. He's not a practicing Jew—although Susan will probably bring him back in. I can see this already because when I recently wanted to give something to Susan and Rob, Susan said, "How about a Chanukah menorah?" I told her to go out and buy anything she wanted, that I would pay for it. Maybe I'm trying harder, going out of my way, going overboard, to make things better than the norm.

When Rob first said Susan was going to convert, I said I would like to get her something. I wanted to get her something personal, a nightgown in her favorite color. I wanted to establish a rapport with her. And I did; I speak to them very often. I don't know her very well yet, but I intend to. Susan is a lovely person. She's got a mind of her own, and she knows what she wants. I think she'll be a good influence on Rob. She should know that we are with her.

THIRTEEN

The Violinist Whose Mother Asked, "Why Can't You Be More Like the Jews?"

Joanna's Journey Home

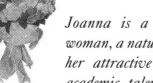

Joanna is a very striking-looking woman, a natural redhead, but despite her attractive appearance, obvious academic talents and great musical gifts, she seemed to lack confidence and self-assurance the day she first appeared in my office. You could tell that she was very sensitive and that her life had been hard. There were many stumbling blocks in her past. Mark, her Jewish fiancé, was very supportive of her effort to learn about Judaism.

I noted that at our very first lesson she already demonstrated a tremendous knowledge of the Bible. She took her studies very seriously. During the unit on prayer she wrote, "Oh Lord, show me the path whereon to walk." Her questioning into the roots of Jewish tradition, her desire to plumb the depths, fascinated me. When she converted to Judaism, she thought

very carefully about choosing her Hebrew name.
Finally she chose the name Yael, meaning to ascend.
It's a very powerful name. And ascend she did. She
felt that the learning process brought her to a whole
new level of being, to a new height of worthiness.

Joanna and Mark's wedding was beautiful—
small, simple, everything according to Jewish law. It
was filled with the warmth of the love between the two
of them. It was definitely Joanna's style: Musicians
played; a garden lay just outside. After the marriage,
I suggested that Joanna pursue an advanced degree in
Judaic studies—I put the idea in her head. That was
because she intensely loved to study the Bible; she got
into it with such a fervor. I was so proud to learn a
few years later that she earned her master's degree in
Judaic studies from Baltimore Hebrew College.

Joanna Tells Her Story

The bane of my existence was to try to please my mother. I started violin lessons at age eight. "Why can't you be more like the Jews?" she would ask. "The Jews work hard, never give up, make good grades and practice their instruments all the time."

She would name some Jewish kid. "Look, he's going places," she would say. "You're just being lazy, squandering your talent." I had always wanted to be Jewish. Sometimes I felt really lousy about being a gentile. I may have been somewhat mad at God because I felt that being born a Jew carried more privilege in God's eyes. The Tanakh (Bible) says God's laws are written in the heart of a Jew.

As a violinist I had a lot of Jewish friends all through school. I often went to synagogue with them and had positive feelings about Jews and Judaism. Jews had an optimistic view of their lives, even though their ancestors had been through a lot of troubles. I was attracted to their lifestyle, to the kind of people they were. When you're brought up Jewish, the sanctity of life is such an important value—it's a revolutionary idea really. Wherever Judaism goes in the world, God's light shines through—and sanity. I thought it was fabulous that Jewish people knew how their lineage worked, where they came from, even though they were dispersed throughout the world. To me that was pretty miraculous, very impressive. Yet the more I was around Jews, the more I realized that I was a gentile. Just because I'm in the apple cart, that doesn't make me an apple.

I converted to Judaism to be in unity with my

husband, Mark, who is Jewish. We had fallen in love and wanted a life together. At first Mark didn't want me to bother converting. He had grown up in the Conservative tradition, but like many children of the 1960s became disillusioned with his upbringing. He was actually looking for more spiritual intimacy than what he had known. His first wife was a nonobservant Jew. While his daughter had a Bat Mitzvah, his sons never went to religious school. But I kept bringing up the idea of my converting to Judaism. Solidarity and peace in a household are very important to me.

I played the violin at a lot of weddings and felt the traditional Jewish wedding, with a huppah (wedding canopy) and a rabbi, was more authentic and definitely the way to go. Instead of having a priest or minister marry you, you marry each other; the rabbi just officiates. Mark and I are both musicians in the Army. None of the Jewish chaplains would marry us at the military facilities. When the military chaplains turned us down (presumably because I was not Jewish), that only further alienated Mark. But it was the catalyst for me.

Somebody recommended I contact Rabbi Weiss. I had thought that you just go down to the synagogue, take a course for a week or two, and you're Jewish. When you want to be a Methodist you go down to the church, talk to the minister, and then you're in. You get baptized; that's no big deal. Maybe there's a two-week course. I thought not much more was involved in becoming a Jew. Rabbi Weiss assured me that I couldn't just sign up. She told me if I wanted to be married as a Jew, I needed to become Jewish first. The process involved intense study over a period of many months. I didn't anticipate all the time, effort and commitment it takes. I just stumbled into Judaism that way, and I liked what I learned. It's inspirational to be around someone like Rabbi Weiss. All of her students benefit from seeing her great strength, because she makes you feel like you, too, can go another mile today.

During World War II my father was a bomber pilot in the Air Force and my mother was a drill sergeant in the Marine Corps. She ran our home as if we were a barracks. (Kids in the neighborhood would tease me that she wore combat boots.) At an early age I had to do humble household chores like dusting, clearing the table, washing and drying the dishes. My mother would say, "Today we're going to have a white-glove inspection." It was pretty mind-boggling because I was only six or seven, and she would run a white glove under the tables to see if I had removed all the dust. I did the best job I could, but I always failed the inspections. It left me feeling anxious all the time. You want to please your parents.

My becoming a Jew was not a problem for my family, even though I grew up in the Methodist church, attending every Sunday with both my parents. We lived in communities with Jewish populations. In Houston my next-door neighbor, who was also my best friend, was Jewish. We played constantly and sometimes I went to synagogue with her. Often I ate at her house, but it wasn't easy because they kept kosher. At five or six, I didn't understand why no milk was served with dinner. I thought they were deprived or something.

As a child I was subject to my mother's tirades and efforts to humiliate me, like putting me in diapers. I guess I wasn't the kind of personality that she could deal with easily. I was gregarious and active; she wanted me to be passive. I didn't fit her mold. My drawers were messy; my closet was messy. She would take a drawer out, dump all the contents on the floor, put the timer on, and say I had fifteen minutes to straighten it or she would wear me out with a spanking. She said she was a failure as a mother if our performance wasn't up to a certain standard. There was this book about two Joannas—a bad Joanna and a good one. My mom would tell me to go read it. I used to read it to myself all the time, hoping the good Joanna's qualities would rub off on me and, in fact, I would try to memorize her good qualities. She was a helper, she was obedient and she didn't complain. If my brother, my sister and I acted up, my mother said we were acting like animals. She made us sit in the dog bed naked or in our underpants for hours. She said we had to remain there until we learned not to act like an animal. If we told a lie (and at age six sometimes you don't even know it's lying), she would put a couple of drops of Tabasco sauce on our tongues and not let us soothe it for an hour. "Liars burn in hell; this is what it's like," she would say. That was worse than any spanking. There were such severe penalties for infractions, no matter how large or small.

After the physical punishment she wouldn't talk to us for days. If I got down on my knees and begged her forgiveness, that sometimes worked. "I'm sorry, Mom," I'd say. "Yeah, you're a very sorry human being," she'd answer. That is really the worst kind of abuse, because it's your parents withdrawing their love from you; I just wanted to be loved.

My father left early in the morning and was gone all day. By the time he came home, the tirades were over and everything was cleaned up. We didn't tell him about it. We thought it was our fault, that we deserved the punishment she meted out. The last thing we wanted to do was to make my mother look bad. We accepted the blame and internalized the guilt. I thought all the time that this is how it is, this is normal. But I wanted to be with my friends because their mothers were nicer. By the time I was fourteen, I was withdrawn and insecure. When you're sent to school worrying about being punished, you can't concentrate. I was always wondering, *What's Mother going to be mad about today?*

When we later moved to Illinois, I wound up going to a high school where the dominant population was Jewish. The Jewish kids were the achievers, and I wanted to be an achiever too. (It must have stuck in my mind to be more like the Jews.) And I liked the Jewish religion itself—it seemed real. It wasn't philosophy or ideology; it was a believable religion of action.

The high school orchestra director saw that I had potential and reached through the clouds that were around me. He started encouraging me, giving me things to practice. The more I practiced, the less my mother hassled me. (I wish I had figured that out earlier.) I was that much closer to fulfilling her vicarious dream of being a professional musician.

I made good enough grades to win a scholarship

to college in the Midwest, but after two years I transferred to the Eastman School of Music in Rochester, New York. I lost interest in organized religion, though I continued to believe strongly in God. At twenty-one, I was reading a few chapters of the Bible every day for about thirty minutes. That gave me an inside view of God's character as well as the history of the Jewish people. So many of the ideas that I formerly had about God were debunked by my Bible-reading. My mother had brought me up in fear of God, always threatening me to get down on my knees. God was the Super Policeman. As I read the Bible, I began to see that God's idea is to be friends with people and to have companionship with us.

At this point I was coming into contact with Jewish musicians, mostly nonobservant Jews. They were undirected, confused by life's usual disappointments and heartaches. I would say, "You're a Jew; pay attention to that; it's something good to be." I was like an emissary. I would tell them to go back to their Jewish roots. Usually I struck a home run. What I said resonated with them.

At Eastman I met my first husband, Harold. He was a gifted opera singer, a tenor. I was so sheltered I had hardly dated. Harold had a lot of enthusiasm and that was what attracted me to him. One day he decided that we should get married. I knew I couldn't trust him—he told lies—and he had an obsession with pornography. I wasn't sure that I loved him, but I was graduating from college and didn't want to go home. Harold seemed to be able to make decisions for me. (I was used to people doing that.) As far as his lack of character in certain areas, I believed in forgiveness and that he would grow up and change. My father didn't want us to get married, so we just eloped. I was almost twenty-two.

After we got married, I realized I had merely exchanged tormentors. Harold flunked out of school—he couldn't finish anything due to fear of failure. Then he wanted to go to Bible college in Florida to become a Christian minister, so we went there. But just before school started, Harold said God told him we should move back to New York and start a church in Rochester. I believed him. My whole upbringing conditioned me to believe that when a person needs to justify their misbehavior, it's much easier to invoke the name of God. My mother and father were always so convinced that God was talking to them. Now here's God telling someone else—never me!—what God's plan was for my life. So we went back to New York, and it was a catastrophe there too, except for the fact that our daughter was born.

Harold used this "I should be a minister" thing to keep from going to work. I supported us by teaching violin lessons privately. Any time Harold had the opportunity to get a good job, he sabotaged it. The pattern would repeat time and again through seventeen years of marriage.

Harold grew tired of never having any money and living from hand to mouth. He went to audition for solo singing roles in Las Vegas. The church was set aside. We spent two and a half years in Las Vegas, where I played in the orchestra at Caesar's Palace—but Harold never found work. Then Harold said God wanted us to move to Europe so he could sing in the opera there. He sang for the biggest agent in Vienna and was told he needed to learn German. But he was so fearful of failure, he never went back. Meanwhile, I played violin in the opera in Italy.

In the 1980s, we returned to America to again start a church in Texas. But the churches all floundered because we couldn't attract enough people. I never told anyone about Harold's problems with pornography and his deepening interest in bondage. His mother had punished him by tying electric cords around him. I was a redhead like she was. He told me that I was his wife and had to accept his authority even if I hated it. I thought of leaving him, but I had our child and I was afraid my parents would say "I told you so" because they didn't want me to get married in the first place. The whole world I had created, the whole appearance of our family, would have dissolved if the truth came to light. People would have shunned us. Such things are not palatable.

Harold got involved with other women. He said I was suspicious and demanding, and if I were more attentive to him he wouldn't need others. I was at a loss as to what to do. I felt powerless. Every time I thought about getting professional help, Harold would say that Christians don't do that; it's a crutch, and if you can't go to God about it, who could you go to? It's a stalwart thing for many people. You just don't talk about your problems to anybody.

The long and the short of it is, Harold was always looking for his big break, and I was always looking for him to grow up. He's a pitiful guy whose dreams have never come true. I paid the ultimate price for it because he blamed me.

The light began to shine in my life around 1986. There was an opening in the Army band in the violin section. I auditioned and got it. I started to feel like a human being, a person who had some worth. I began to see that I had been in denial about my marriage; I realized I had been avoiding responsibility myself by not confronting the pain and Harold's unseemliness.

Harold had hit me from the beginning. I'd go to work with bruises on my arms (not on the face—though he had smacked me in the face several times and broken my glasses); in the locker room, the women would ask me what was wrong with my arm. I lied, made up excuses.

Then one day I just woke up. Harold had always said if I ever tried to walk out on him, he'd break my arm so I couldn't play the violin. I knew that if I left him, I'd have to leave secretly. I paid rent for an apartment, but didn't move in for a number of months. Then on Veterans Day, November 12, 1991, I just got in the car at 5 A.M. and left—and never went back.

After leaving home, I had gone to the band in tears, wearing sunglasses, but nobody seemed to notice but Mark. He was the band's head arranger. He just made himself available as a friend and listener. I wasn't suicidal, but I was despairing of life. I had done the victim thing—constant internal pity—for years. It becomes part of your psychological makeup. It was affecting my playing and my performing—like having ten thousand monkeys on your back that you need to pry off one by one. It takes a lot of energy. I didn't want to go through that anymore. Nor was I interested in revenge against my husband—I just wanted to be free. I began to see doctors and it was helpful. Mark and I eventually fell in love and wanted a life together. My daughter went into the military to win my approval, to sort of emulate me. I don't see her too often because she is in Georgia, but we are close.

After a year of study, I chose a Conservative conversion to Judaism. I talked to the Bet Din (rabbinical court) and then went to the mikvah (ritual bath) and said prayers. I really enjoyed it. When I got out of the water, I felt like a new person, like I was a part of Israel, the collective people of Israel. Mark's parents were very supportive; they seemed to think it was the right thing to do.

My family was completely happy for me. They thought our wedding was beautiful. Friends of mine, a string trio from the Army band, played music. All my siblings were there. My brother held up one of the huppah (wedding canopy) poles. My daughter was glad that I was happy and away from her father. My ex-husband wrote my parents a letter saying that by converting to Judaism and marrying a non-Christian, I was losing my salvation. But all my dad cared about was that I was happy.

I had converted to Judaism, but it wasn't enough for me. I wanted to know more. I decided to pursue a master's degree in Judaic studies at Baltimore Hebrew University. It took me four years to earn it. I had to study part-time at night, one course at a time.

The summer of 1994 I was in a bad car accident. To avoid hitting another car, I swerved off the road and hit a tree. The airbag broke my bow arm. It was a very bad fracture requiring surgery, two plates and twelve screws. I couldn't play violin for a number of months and struggled with intense pain for about two years due to nerve damage. I thought my career with the violin might come to an end. If I had to move to another career, I wanted it to be something I really liked—Jewish studies. If I got advanced degrees, I would have the option of teaching or doing historical research.

Fortunately my arm got better. Music was still my primary calling. I felt like God had handed back to me the ability to play. Then I felt like taking violin lessons again, which I hadn't done in eighteen years. So I auditioned for a scholarship at a nearby university and was accepted. Now I am working toward completing my doctorate in violin. I think I'm a better, stronger violinist now; there's more intelligence to my playing, and more passion, more abandon. My playing reflects the greater confidence I have in myself, arising from the very positive, encouraging aspects of Judaism and the Jewish people I've known—like my husband and my professors. The Jewish people's attitude has always been that it's a very positive experience to learn something. That is a lot of what I got out of studying with other Jewish students.

Practicing Judaism just feels right to me, participating in Sukkot and Passover, etc. We attend seder, I'll prepare a Shabbat dinner. Mark is agreeable now, not reluctant like he used to be. Since I've become a Jew he has become more animated and more interested in Judaism. Mark was a little tainted by what he perceived as hypocrisy in the synagogue; I feel like I've helped him understand that it has nothing to do with Judaism, but with a particular individual being hypocritical. He attends synagogue with me at Fort Belvoir, but when I was going to Baltimore Hebrew University, we went together to programs at an Orthodox synagogue, and he seemed to really enjoy them.

I feel my identity is different now. I identify with the travails of the Jewish people and the whole Sinai sojourn experience; I feel a kinship with Jews throughout the ages, since they left Egypt. And I feel a kinship with Jewish string players I'm in contact with. They feel wonderful about my becoming a Jew;

they feel validated. Some don't practice their faith, so they're inspired when they see a former gentile get so interested in something they've left behind. It stimulates them to go back to it.

I've come to understand in a way I didn't comprehend before just how isolated in the world the Jewish people have felt, and how the Christian populace has often denied their worth. Mark has helped me. I couldn't believe that at Easter time in Pittsburgh, where he grew up, he had to run away from Christian kids chasing him for killing Jesus. And within the last decade, at a funeral he attended, the priest was touting the same old theology. When I see injustice, misery and meanness, sometimes I feel like Job who said he wished he hadn't been born. David, Elijah, Job—they all went through troubles. The Bible says God's ears are always open to our cries. I just cry out, asking God to have mercy. And God is merciful in small ways. There are people who help relieve suffering all over the world. It's just not always very visible. (The Israelis have sent rescue teams to countries in need, including those that hate them.)

I feel like I'm a better person now just from being with Mark. There's a gentleness in my husband that stems from Judaism. Mark is such a wonderful husband. He is sincere and the most devoted man I've ever known—to me, his children and his parents. Work is not at the top of his list; it's people that he cares about. He created a safe environment for me, enabling my real personality to emerge. Our relationship has gotten really good. He thinks I'm funny, and that makes me happy. I'm in love, I'm content, I'm at peace. Before I met Mark I felt like I was merely existing, just hanging on. When I found him, I felt like my life just got started.

Mark's Conclusion

Before we even discussed it, Joanna took the initiative to convert to Judaism. One day she just said, "I'm looking into this." My sense is that it was something she felt compelled to do. It takes a great deal of commitment to go through with it.

Joanna was pretty knowledgeable even before she started studying. She's expanded her knowledge greatly. I found myself picking up things when she was getting her training. I would attend a lecture with her, see the Jewish environment she was in. The experiences she received—I made them my experiences, too. Of course, anything you can share like that makes you feel more bonded together, stronger as a couple. Judaism is a major thing to be sharing.

FOURTEEN

A Short History of Conversion to Judaism

Imagine a debate occurring almost twenty-five hundred years ago in the city of Jerusalem. Ezra the Scribe has determined that the marriage of Jewish men to gentile wives in the small and struggling Jewish community poses a problem demanding immediate redress. What was happening at that point in Jewish history that sparked such an attitude? Jews returning from exile and striving to rebuild their homeland were abandoning the One God and being lured into the worship of other gods introduced by their gentile wives. No less than the future of Judea and the Judeans was at stake, so Ezra decreed that the gentile wives must go.

But at other points in Jewish history the response to intermarriage was completely different. Much earlier, for example, our faith attracted many individuals through marriage, like Moses' wife and Joseph's wife, who were welcomed with open arms and granted full membership in the community. These converts coming into Judaism were multiethnic, yet they took on Jewish memory and identified themselves with the fathers and mothers of Israel. They adopted the history of the Jewish people as their own spiritual history, beginning with Abraham, who left his father's house and religion to follow God to a new land, and Sarah, who followed her man and embraced his faith. Such converts developed a sense of completeness when they absorbed the culture and traditions of the Jews.

Many famous individuals throughout Jewish history were converts, for example, the prophet Ovadiah, whose prophesy was included in the Hebrew Bible. Other scholars, authorities within the Talmud, were either referred to as converts or children of converts, such as the famous and admired rabbis Rabbi Meir and Rabbi Akiva. Such individuals contributed to the mainstream of Jewish history, and their very existence should encourage other converts to follow in their footsteps.

So which is it? Does Judaism look for converts? Does it strive to change people's hearts and minds and lead them down the way of the Jewish faith? Or is Judaism a nonconverting religion that even intentionally pushes converts away? Can Judaism be considered a missionary religion, or is it a religion that looks with apprehension at the entry of others into the family of the Jewish people? A glance at the history of conversion in Judaism reveals that the answer is mixed. There is definitely a dichotomy within Jewish tradition. At any given point in Jewish history, Jews either discouraged or encouraged conversion. Perhaps the events occurring at a particular time and place helped shape the attitude. Let's take a look at the way the rabbis over the centuries have interpreted the activities of Abraham and Sarah as described in the following scripture: "And Abram took Sarai his wife, and Lot his brother's son, and all their substance that they had gathered, and the souls they had gotten in Haran; and they went forth to go into the land of Canaan; and into the land of Canaan, they came" (Gen. 12:5).

The biblical narrative makes it clear that there was a diverse group of people from a multitude of backgrounds who settled with Abraham and Sarah in the land of Canaan. They formed a framework of community, and to make that community cohesive they developed an organized system of leadership under Abraham. The rabbis of the early centuries of the common era took the word "souls" to mean the proselytes (followers or converts) whom Abraham made among the men and Sarah made among the women. These individuals became subservient to God's law and followed the Almighty in a spiritual adventure. Abraham and Sarah were the first man and woman to spread the belief in One God and were able to change people's hearts and minds and direct them toward the faith in which they believed.

God's choice of Abraham was apparently no arbitrary election. The image of the patriarch Abraham is of someone who opened his tent to the four corners of the earth and encouraged others to become, like him, a believer in One God. Of course, at the beginning of Jewish history to convert did not mean to become Jewish, because such a concept did not yet exist. A believer in One God was the ideology that Abraham represented.

Later in Jewish history, Jethro, father-in-law of Moses and a priest of Midian, is considered by the rabbis to be a convert. Moses welcomed him, and Jethro accepted the beliefs of his son-in-law, Moses. The non-Jews who accompanied the children of Israel out of Egypt—the mixed multitude present at Sinai—were similarly assimilated into the Jewish people. And when the children of Israel conquered the Promised Land of Canaan, those people who remained within the Holy Land also accepted the authority of the Jews and their belief in One God.

Consider the history of King David, one of the most important figures in Jewish life—past, present and future. The great-grandmother of King David was Ruth, a convert to Judaism. Ruth went with her mother-in-law, Naomi, and accepted the Jewish way of life. She vowed that Naomi's people would be her people, Naomi's God would be her God, and wherever she would go, Ruth would go with her. Ruth becomes the great-grandmother of David and the great-great-grandmother of King Solomon. Ruth's conversion is treated from a positive perspective, so much so that David's memorial day on Shavuot is celebrated by reading the Scroll of Ruth in public as part of the service.

During the rule of the Hasmonean dynasty in the second century B.C.E., John Hyracanus conquered the land of the Edomites in the southern part of Judea and compelled the inhabitants to convert. The Hasmonean rulers of Judea taught Jewish values and traditions to all those who would listen and did what was necessary to bring as many people into Judaism as possible—which made Judaism the dominant religion in the region. But the Hasmonean kingdom was

torn apart by fighting over the throne by two brothers. The Edomites who had been forcibly converted
took over the throne with the help of the Romans.
Antipater, an Edomite, welcomed Roman intervention and ruled with their help. Herod, his son, married Miriam, a descendant of the Hasmoneans, but
then ordered her killed. Obviously, the behavior of
these Edomite converts, Antipater and Herod,
aroused suspicion of converts in general and helped
generate a negative attitude toward conversion.

During Roman times Jews generally felt that
Judaism could not be accepted as a universal religion.
All of God's laws or commandments manifest in the
Torah were directed at the Jews alone. Other people
could disregard the dietary laws, the laws regarding
purity, the Sabbath, etc., and could still have a right
to the world to come if they were decent, civilized
human beings. Still, many Romans and other gentiles
were attracted to Judaism and did, in fact, convert.
They appreciated Judaism's sacred books and the
belief in One God, and they respected the history of
the Jews.

At first Jews and Judaism were tolerated by Rome,
but soon Roman legislation would prohibit Judaism
from spreading. Converting to Judaism came to be
viewed as a threat to Roman religion and to the

emperors who claimed to be gods themselves. In 339 C.E., the first Christian emperor also prohibited Jews from receiving converts. Marriages between Jews and Christians were outlawed, with the consequences of converting to Judaism resulting in confiscation of property or death. Jews and Judaism were tolerated only because of the hope that they would eventually learn more of Christianity and convert to the Christian way of life. With such an attitude on the part of their rulers in both the pre-Christian and Christian worlds, it is little wonder that Jews developed a wariness of conversion. Conversion jeopardized the entire community, a community already struggling to exist in a non-Jewish-majority world.

Within the Talmud itself can be found two opposite approaches to conversion. One school of thought welcomes converts; the other pushes them away. Each side feels strongly. There were rabbis who feared that converts would be more pious than Jews born into Judaism, which by contrast would hurt the born Jews in the eyes of God. The positive approach states that Jews were dispersed throughout the world because God wants to spread Judaism and have gentiles join the Jewish faith and become part of the Jewish people.

The Talmud also relates the famous story of Hillel and Shammai. We learn how patiently Hillel welcomed the potential convert who asked him to teach him the entire Torah while he stood on one foot. Shammai, however, pushed this potential convert away with his rod. Hillel shows kindness; he is friendly and truly interested in those who want to become a part of the Jewish people. Even if the motives are in question, Hillel tells the potential convert to go and study. On the other hand, Shammai is not as tolerant and has little or no patience. He drives the potential convert away if he suspects his motives or sincerity. Hillel's method, nurturing and welcoming, brings in a new fully observant Jew to Judaism. I believe he should serve as a role model for today. However, there are many rabbis who continue the Talmudic tradition of challenging potential converts, warning them that Jews are a persecuted people who have suffered throughout the generations. But the sincere convert rises to the occasion and withstands the rebuff.

A historical and influential set of guidelines dealing with conversion was codified by the famous philosopher–physician Maimonides (1135–1204) in his Mishnah Torah. His ruling was followed by rabbis for generations. He states that if a man or woman has no ulterior motive for becoming a convert, he or she should be examined further. They cannot be considered for conversion if they want material gain, or if they want an Israelite woman or man for the prospect of marriage. If severe screening was complete, and if the potential convert came out of love and devotion, then he or she would be accepted into the family of Judaism. Once converted, the convert was to be extended full rights. Thus, sincere motivation on the part of the potential convert was the basic criterion for accepting an individual.

The fact that during the Middle Ages Jews jeopardized their lives and property by accepting proselytes at all leads one to believe they regarded conversion as part of the commandment to love the proselyte. There were always those who managed to convert under the most dire of circumstances. Some were former clergymen whose studies led them to choose Judaism. Many through the centuries died for this choice; some even burned at the stake. In Spain around the turn of the fifteenth century, during the time of the Marranos, secret Jews were forced to become Christians outwardly, and the rabbis were much more lenient about conversion because so many Jews had been lost to Christianity. The rabbis tried to do whatever they could to encourage those who wanted to come back to or into Judaism.

The Torah tells us of three commandments of love: love of God, love of the friend or neighbor, and love of the *ger*—the proselyte, the one who comes to dwell with you. It is a mitzvah or commandment to love the proselyte, to pray for him or her and to lend help in any way that is possible. For two thousand years Jews have prayed every day, within the heart of the Jewish prayer service, for the Righteous, the Pious and the Just Converts. These are the important people for whom prayers must be said.

In the modern era, significant losses were suffered by the Jewish people during the Holocaust. Intermarriage and secularization further imperil the survival of Judaism. On the one hand, we Jews have been encouraged to participate as full members of a community, but this full participation leads to interacting with non-Jews and ultimately a loss of Jewish identification. In the early 1900s, there were large pockets of Jewish communities where Jews lived together, worshiped together and practiced customs and traditions easily. They were able to meet other Jews and create new Jewish homes. Today Jews are spread throughout the world and most often live as assimilated individuals. In the United States especially, most Jews no longer live in ghetto-type communities where they see themselves bound to Jewish tradition. In fact, the path for marrying someone outside of Judaism is now a way of life for the majority of U.S. Jews. Universities and other institutions, which once accepted only a token number of Jews, today open their doors, placing young Jews in an environment conducive to meeting and marrying outside the Jewish faith.

Yet the mates of intermarried Jews offer a potential rebuilding of the Jewish people and a rekindling of the Jewish spirit for future generations. How should we react when potential converts come knocking at our doors? Think of someone climbing a mountain. We must give a hand whenever necessary to help them reach their destination. Converts find the road to Judaism very difficult in certain stages, and without love, devotion and understanding they will never get there. Our leaders must convey the message that Judaism cares about converts. We must reach into our tradition and seize and elevate those elements that open the door. We must look to the example of Abraham, our patriarch, whose tent was always open on all four sides to welcome those who chose to enter. That must be how our era hails the convert and potential convert.

Finally, those who choose a Jewish way of life must be embraced and welcomed into the community and encouraged to become involved in whatever capacity appeals to them. A positive attitude on the part of the community is needed if we are to succeed in preserving our tradition by adding the commitment and enrichment of converts. If we fail to welcome potential converts with sincere motivation, born Jews who care about perpetuating Judaism may have no answer to the painful question, "How will we bring our heritage into the next millennium?"

SUMMARY

Over the years, Rabbi Bernice K. Weiss has shepherded hundreds of students into the family of the Jewish people. For most, the interest in Judaism is sparked by a decision to marry a Jewish man or woman. But that is only the beginning. In the gentle hands of a teacher who has witnessed and understands their turmoil, their conflicts, their tears, they bare their personal struggles. What emerge are amazing, even powerful, soul-stirring stories of re-creation —the extraordinary adventure of becoming a Jew at the turn of the twenty-first century.

An Asian-American whose father owns a Japanese restaurant marries a secular Jew but leads him to Orthodox Judaism; a Belgian raised by nuns meets a Jew and finds her faith in Israel; a former Christian Sunday school teacher from a small farm town falls in love with a Jewish girl and with her faith as well; an African-American woman lawyer, a Harvard graduate, discovers Judaism and keeps kosher in a small southern town: their varied stories and eight more are revealed in these pages.

The twists and turns and the directions their lives ultimately take are a source of inspiration to those contemplating Judaism, and to all in search of faith. They are a gift to the Jewish people.